LET ROME
SPEAK FOR HERSELF

LET ROME
SPEAK FOR HERSELF

John Edward Millheim, Editor

Regular Baptist Press
1300 North Meacham Road
Post Office Box 95500
Schaumburg, Illinois 60195

Library of Congress Cataloging in Publication Data
  Main entry under title:

Let Rome speak for herself.

    Rev. ed. of: Let Rome speak for herself/Robert T. Ketcham. 1956
    Bibliography: p.
    Contents: Authority/James R. Lytle—The Eucharist and the Mass/James R. Lytle—The Sacraments/James R. Lytle—[etc.]
    1. Catholic Church—Doctrinal and controversial works—Protestant authors—Addresses, essays, lectures.
I. Millheim, John Edward. II. Lytle, James Russell.
III. Jarvis, Charles Everett. IV. Ketcham, Robert Thomas, 1889-1978. Let Rome speak for herself.
BX1765.2.L47 1982   282   82-16616
ISBN 0-87227-890-0

LET ROME SPEAK FOR HERSELF
© 1982
Regular Baptist Press
Printed in U.S.A.

Contributors

CHARLES EVERETT JARVIS, B.S., M.Div.

B.S. Ohio State University; M.Div., Baptist Bible School of Theology (*Cum Laude*); Th.M. Candidate Baptist Bible School of Theology; Associate Pastor, Fellowship Baptist Church, Upper Marlboro, Maryland.

JAMES RUSSELL LYTLE, B.R.E., M.Div.

State University of New York; B.R.E., Baptist Bible College; M.Div., Baptist Bible School of Theology (*Cum Laude*); Th.M. Candidate, Baptist Bible School of Theology; Instructor, Baptist Bible College.

Editor

JOHN EDWARD MILLHEIM, B.A., M.Div., Th.M., D.D.

Vice President, Graduate Division, Baptist Bible School of Theology. Diploma, Philadelphia College of Bible; B.A., Houghton College; M.Div., Faith Theological Seminary; Th.M., Princeton Theological Seminary; Graduate Studies, Drew University; Goethe Institute, Murnau, Germany; Pastor, 8 years; Administrator, American Council of Christian Churches, 7 years; Assistant Professor, Baptist Bible College, 4 years. School of Theology; 1973—

Contents

Preface

The pages which follow in this volume had their beginning in 1981 with a conversation I had with the Reverend James F. Dersham, Managing Editor of Publications of the Regular Baptist Press. Our conversation centered around the updating of Robert T. Ketcham's booklet, *Let Rome Speak for Herself.*[1] I suggested to Mr. Dersham the use of several Th.M. candidates at Baptist Bible School of Theology, Clarks Summit, Pennsylvania, in the field of Historical Theology to work along with me in the updating and enlarging of this former work. The suggestion met enthusiastically with Mr. Dersham's approval and for the past year serious attention and work has been given to this task. I might also add that it has been a real challenge and delight to work alongside these seminary students.

It has always been a strong conviction of mine that not only does the seminary need the Church but the Church needs the seminary. The seminary must not only be looked upon as a source of manpower, but also of manuscripts. There is a great need for the theological personnel in the seminary to do some community exegesis, as well as joint projects, with oversight and direction of students from those who teach them. The results of this type of research should be made available to a wider audience. Thus not only will the scholars of this community be strengthened and helped, but the churches as well.

The material set forth in this particular work is the result of many hours of discussion, writing, rewriting, checking of sources, debate and consultation. It really is an experiment in utilizing keen seminarians in a research project under a general editor. Both James Lytle and Charles Jarvis have labored long in their research and writing to bring together a well-documented treatment from Catholic sources of Rome's position today. As you will see, it has not changed significantly since the Council of Trent (1545-63).[2] While the appearance of change has come about since Vatican II (1962– 65),[3] one will find that very little as far as the major teachings of the Roman Catholic church have changed and thus are still binding upon her members.

The position of the Roman Catholic church with respect to her cardinal doctrines remains unaltered. While one sees changes in attitude toward the "separated brethren," the position of the Roman Catholic church with respect to the materials set forth in each chapter of this volume, reaffirms the unchangeableness of her official position on doctrine.[4]

The purpose of all of this research is to bring to the reader the official sources from which these doctrines had been derived. While much more material could be cited, there has been an attempt to center our attention on the key statements in the documents so that we might get to the heart of the church's affirmations.

While this treatment is much longer than the former booklet, it is done with the intention to make the sources available to the reader. To present past affirmations along with present reaffirmations requires more time and space. It is the desire of both the contributors as well as the editor that this present work will serve as a useful document in a better understanding of where the church of Rome stands when she speaks for herself in the areas covered within the chapters of this book.

John Edward Millheim
Clarks Summit, Pennsylvania
June, 1982

---

1. R. T. Ketcham, *Let Rome Speak for Herself* (Chicago: Regular Baptist Press, 1956).

2. J. D. Douglas, General Editor, *The New International Dictionary of the Christian Church* (Grand Rapids, Michigan: Zondervan Publishing House, 1974), pp. 984, 195.

3. Ibid., pp. 1012-1014.

4. Walter Abbott, Ed., *The Documents of Vatican II* (New York: The American Press, 1966), p. 354.

Introduction

T he entire thrust, design and purpose of this particular work is
to do exactly what the title suggests. It is important for
purposes presented in this work to "let Rome speak for herself."
This is why first-hand documents and sources have been used in
order to do that very thing.

On the 12th of March, 1981, I attended a lecture at Kings'
College in Wilkes-Barre, Pennsylvania. The distinguished speaker
at that occasion was Avery Dulles, S. J., the theme of his address
was "Who Speaks for the Church?" When touching on the subject
of the official teaching body of the church which consists of popes,
bishops, and their appointed spokesmen, he stated "their primary
task is to perpetuate the apostolic witness—to preserve, transmit
and defend the faith delivered to the church by its Lord. In their
official pronouncements, when they speak in their capacity as
spokesmen for the faith, these pastoral authorities take pains not to
teach their own private opinions, but to articulate what has always
been, at least implicitly, the faith of the church itself. They
frequently use expressions such as 'the church teaches,' 'the church
believes,' 'the church confesses.'

"We may conclude, then," says Dulles, "that the pastor
magisterium, when it lives up to its responsibilities, does speak for
the Catholic Church."

Dulles is careful to emphasize that it is not self-evident that in
every individual case the popes and bishops of the past or present
have succeeded in speaking for the church. He has suggested that
there is a need for additional signs to show that they have measured
up to their responsibility. In the final thesis of his address, he
proposes the following: "The claims of popes and bishops to speak

authentically for the church must be made good. What assurances do we have that in a given case their teaching is indeed authentic in the sense of being valid and true?

"To be Catholic is to have a certain general trust in the church and in its acknowledged leaders, including especially those who speak for the church officially. In view of their training, the position in the community, and the advice available to them, they are in a good position to speak for the church. Catholics believe, in addition, that the Lord has promised to be with those who have the responsibility to teach authoritatively in His name. Together with their office they receive a special charisma or assistance from the Holy Spirit to be reliable teachers, so that in hearing them the faithful may hear Christ Himself. A doctrine, therefore, has special weight if it is known to have the authority of the ecclesiastical magisterium behind it."

I have quoted from Avery's speech only to lay some groundwork for how the official documents in this volume should be received by the average Roman Catholic within his church. One certainly would not say in light of Dulles' speech that the Documents of Trent or those of Vatican II, or the various catechisms would be someone's own private interpretation, but rather teachings which have the authority of the ecclesiastical officials behind them. Hence, the average Catholic must trust in his leaders and his church and that these documents are reliable and trustworthy as authentic, official teachings for him to follow. This is the very heart of what this volume is seeking to present and why these documents are in conflict with the teaching of the Holy Scripture.

This conflict is not new, of course. Luther struck a major blow at official Roman Catholic doctrine when he reported the happenings at Augsburg in the *Acta Augustana* (WA[1] 2.6–26; English: LW[2] 31.259–292). It was on October 15, 1518, that Luther encountered Cardinal Cajetanus, an official representative of the pope. Luther's writings and pronouncements had stirred a great deal of controversy and hence, Cajetanus was coming to appeal to Luther to do several things for the Holy Father in Rome. The first thing that he was asked was that he speak the simple word "revoco" (I recant); and then, that he promise not to teach novelties again; and finally, that he resolve never again to disturb the peace of the holy church. Luther was thoroughly aghast at this ultimatum and meekly he begged to be shown his errors, saying that he was not personally aware of any.

Augsburg, like Gettysburg, was a three days battle. Of the issues discussed, one loomed large above all others. That issue was the problem of authority. Luther was ultimately driven to say that there have indeed been some teachings by the popes, some utterances from the church's magisterium that have been patently false, measured against the clear witness of Scripture. Luther maintained that that should surprise no one. Peter erred and was reprimanded by Paul, and the successors of Peter likewise had erred when they had departed from the truth of the gospel. Luther's major axiom was that only those decrees of popes which were proven to be in agreement with Holy Scripture deserved to be believed, and that no papal teaching should be left untested.

Luther held to this position when he debated Eck at Leipzig. He said, "It is not in the power of the Roman Pontiff or of the Inquisitors of heresy to establish new articles of faith, but only to judge according to those established. Nor can any professing Christian be compelled to believe whatever is beyond Holy Scripture" (WA³ 2.279). For Luther, then, his preference was the final and complete authority of Scripture as the judge of all doctrine. In this Leipzig debate Luther said of Eck, "The learned Doctor, I grieve to say, penetrates the Scriptures as profoundly as a water spider does the water, yet he flees from the face of them (the Scriptures) as the devil flees from the Cross. With all reverence for the Fathers, I prefer the authority of the Scriptures and commend them to the future judges of this debate." Not to be outdone by Luther, Eck stated of Luther, "The impatient monk is more scurrilous than becomes the gravity of a theologian. He prefers the authority of Scripture to the Fathers and sets himself up as a second Delphic oracle who alone has an understanding of the Scriptures, superior to that of any Father." While this debate ended in bitterness, nevertheless, the point was made. Councils and popes, said Luther, have erred and do err.

The debate that loomed large during the Reformation concerning the issue of authority is still going on today. Shall we trust Scripture alone or popes, bishops and their appointed spokesman? As Evangelicals we have rested our cause with Scripture alone as the complete and trustworthy foundation for faith and practice.

This book intends to show how Roman Catholic doctrine emerges from the Roman Catholic church documents claiming equal authority with Holy Scripture. Luther, with those before and after him, has maintained that Scripture and Scripture alone is our only rule for faith and practice. The conflict that is seen in this volume, then, is between the pronouncements of the official Roman Catholic teachings and the statements of Holy Scripture. Since the official documents of the Roman Catholic church in many places contradict Scripture, we have insisted that in those instances Scripture must be maintained as the only authoritative, inerrant voice in doctrinal matters.

When Luther was asked by Charles V at the Diet of Worms to retract his writings, he delivered this statement which has been quoted over and over again as a great witness that Scripture alone is the only foundation of faith. Luther said, "Since then Your Majesty and Your Lordships desire a simple reply, I will answer without horns and without teeth. Unless I am convicted by Scriptures and plain reason—I do not accept the authority of popes and councils, for they have contradicted each other—my conscience is captive to the Word of God. I cannot and I will not recant anything, for to go against my conscience is neither right nor safe. God help me. Amen."[4]

As you move through this volume and assess the material presented, I am sure you will see that the thrust is to contrast what official Roman Catholic teaching claims as binding on its members with what the Scriptures teach as binding. We have provided a Scriptural rebuttal of those documents where those documents are in direct contradiction with Scripture. Either we must maintain that the Scripture speaks for the church or the documents of Rome speak for the church. It is the thesis of this volume that Scripture, and Scripture alone, is the only foundation for faith and practice. It is upon this singular premise that we present this material which stands in stark contrast to what the Scriptures teach.

John Edward Millheim

1. Luther's Werke, Kritische Gesamtausgabe. (Schriften.) Weimer, p. 1883ff.

2. Luther's Works, American Edition. Edited by J. Pelikan and H. Lehmann. Philadelphia and St. Louis, p. 1955ff.

3. Luther's Werke, Kritische Gesamtausgabe. (Schriften.) Weimer, p. 1883ff.

4. Roland Bainton, *Here I Stand* (Nashville: Abingdon—Cokesbury Press, MCML), p. 185.

1/ Authority

James R. Lytle

Authority as an Issue

The course of church history has demonstrated the fact that the Scriptures provide the foundation for any discussion of doctrine. The difference between any two religious movements quickly reduces to a difference in understanding of the Scripture, or to a difference in interpretive methodology. At first glance, such statements may appear to be an oversimplification of the complex problems of difference in religions throughout the world—but such is not the case.

The Word of God itself claims to be the foundation for all religious practice. In 2 Timothy 3:16 and 17, we read, "All scripture is given by inspiration of God, and is profitable for doctrine, for reproof, for correction, for instruction in righteousness: That the man of God may be perfect, throughly furnished unto all good works." This would be a lofty claim for any other book, but the God-breathed Bible is indeed the foundation upon which all of life is to rest.

In the doctrinal statement of the General Association of Regular Baptist Churches, this affirmation is echoed: "We believe the Bible to be the true center of Christian unity and the supreme standard by which all human conduct, creed, and opinions shall be tried."[1] The Regular Baptist Fellowship has always stood firmly upon the inspiration of the Scriptures, and this has not been an empty theological statement. The Scripture is the bread of life which provides sustenance to the "man of God," and offers him the satisfaction of a God-directed life if only he will study.

The Roman Catholic church makes similar claims for the Scripture. In the documents of the Council of Trent (1545–1563) we read of the foundational teaching of the Roman Catholic church. This teaching is altered but slightly in the Documents of Vatican II, as we shall see:

> The most holy ecumenical and general Synod of Trent . . . following the example of the orthodox fathers . . . receives and venerates with equal devotion and reverence all the books both of the Old and New Testaments (since God is the author of both . . .).[2]

If these words were the only ones penned by Roman authorities at Trent, one could find little difference between the position of orthodoxy espoused by the GARBC and the doctrine of the Roman Catholic church! The strong statement on the origin of the Bible as authored by God is foundational to historic Baptist doctrine and leads to a lifestyle which is completely controlled by the Word of God.

Sadly, the quotation above continues:

> . . . and also said traditions, both those pertaining to faith and those pertaining to morals, as dictated either orally by Christ or by the Holy Spirit and preserved by continuous succession in the Catholic Church . . . .[3]

The Catholic church, while laying claim to the authorship of God in the Scriptures, adds traditions to the Scripture which have evolved since the time of the Scripture, and "receives and reverences" them also with equal authority with the Scripture.

These documents of the Roman Catholic church demonstrate a fundamental difference between the Roman Catholic church's view of Scripture as presented in the documents of Trent and the doctrine of the historic Baptist movement. The Baptist believes that 2 Timothy 3:16 and 17 mandate the exclusivity of the Scriptures in matters of faith and practice. How else could the man of God be "thoroughly furnished unto every good work" but by knowledge of the Scripture?

As stated above, the issue of authority is also a concern of the Second Vatican Council. The Documents of Vatican II do not change the dictums of the Council of Trent. They explain Trent and make twentieth century application of the doctrines of Trent. Consider the following quotation in the matter of inspiration:

> Those divinely revealed realities which are contained and presented in sacred Scripture have been committed to writing under the inspiration

of the Holy Spirit. Holy Mother church, relying on the belief of the apostles, holds that the books of both the Old and New Testament in their entirety, with all their parts, are sacred and canonical because, having been written under the inspiration of the Holy Spirit (cf. John 20:31; 2 Tim. 3:16; 2 Pet. 1:19–21; 3:15, 16) they have God as their author and have been handed on as such to the Church herself. In composing the sacred books, God chose men and while employed by Him they made use of their powers and abilities, so that with Him acting in them and through them, they, as true authors, consigned to writing everything and only those things which He wanted.[4]

As did the Council of Trent, so the Second Vatican Council affirmed the inspiration and divine origin of the Scriptures.

The Conflict of Roman Catholic Tradition and Authority

Though the Documents of Vatican II make no comment in echoing the Trent view of inspiration, they may be presumed to echo the canon of Trent. One also finds a list of those books which were "received by the Synod."[5] Included in that list are books such as Tobit, Judith, Wisdom, Ecclesiasticus, Baruch and the first two of the books of Maccabees.

These apocryphal books were not accepted as Scripture by the Jews of Christ's time, nor by Christ Himself. In His statement about the Scripture (which He maintained as unbreakable in John 10:35), Christ affirmed the content of the Old Testament canon in reference to the "law, prophets, and writings" (Luke 24:44). These are the books which the Jews accepted as Scripture, and they include all of the books of the "Protestant" Old Testament, though they occur in a different order. The "law, prophets, and writings" do not include any of the books listed above which the Council of Trent approved.

This notation is crucial. As stated above, the Bible is the foundation of religious authority. If books are added to the recognized canon, they become authoritative, and their teachings become binding for the Church. The subject of purgatory, which is foreign to the sixty-six book canon, is an admissible doctrine if 2 Maccabees is admitted as Scripture. This subject will receive further treatment later.

To this point, we have noted that a "face value" assessment of the doctrine of inspiration would cause one to perceive great similarities in the "bibliology" of the Roman Catholic church and the GARBC. Closer examination reveals a greater difference between the two groups. Though the Roman church believes in inspiration, they claim inspiration for books which were not recognized by our Lord as canonical while He ministered on earth—though those books were already written. In addition, the Roman church adds a body of writing by the church fathers to the realm of "authoritative." These writings, which were not produced by Christ's apostles, nor under their supervision, are taken with equal authority with the word of Scripture. The Catholic has a wider base of authority than the Christian who holds to an inspired Scripture of sixty-six books. This wider base of authority will make possible the authoritative teaching of doctrines not contained in the "shorter" canon.

It is one thing to know what the bounds of God-breathed writings should be; it is quite another to be able to interpret the writings of Scripture correctly. According to the Documents of the Council of Trent,

> no one relying on his own wisdom in matters of faith and morals that pertain to the upbuilding of Christian doctrine, may twist the Holy Scriptures to his own opinions or presume to interpret Holy Scripture contrary to that sense which Holy Mother church has held and holds, whose right it is to judge concerning the true sense and interpretation of the Holy Scriptures, or contrary to the unanimous tradition of the fathers, even though such interpretations should at no time be intended for publication. Those acting to this shall be reported by the ordinaries and punished with penalties appointed by law.[6]

Certainly no Christian would desire that human opinion would be the final authority in the understanding of Scripture. The shifting sands of human opinion provide no foundation for an understanding of the unchanging Word of God. In the words of the statement above, there is established an unchanging standard for the understanding of the Bible: that which has been interpreted in time past and approved by the Roman church is not subject to further understanding and change.

While the fundamentalist would find this attitude distasteful, he must at least admit that it will cause uniformity in interpretation! The problem of differing interpretations has perplexed Bible scholars for centuries. The believer who accepts the authority of the Word in 2 Timothy 3:16 and 17 must believe that within the Bible itself lie all of the necessary teachings regarding doctrine and practice. In 2 Peter 1:20, the Bible teaches that ". . . no prophecy of the Scripture is of any private interpretation." In other words, Scripture must not be interpreted without regard for the remainder of Scripture. The commonly utilized principle of interpretation, the analogy of faith, states that "the Bible interprets the Bible." If one wished to arrive at an authoritative interpretation of Scripture, he must arrive at that conclusion within the context of the whole of the Word of God. In this manner one may have certainty that he has understood the intent of God and the writer of the Scripture correctly.

God, Who loved the world so much that He gave His only begotten Son to die on the cross for sin, has entrusted His Word to the people for whom Christ died. At no time in the history of the Church has the Word of God been accessible to so many of the people of the world as it is today. In the early days of the Church, the apostles wrote letters to the people of the Church, and fully expected that these people would be able to comprehend the message from God. No external standard was needed for interpretation; those who could understand the language could understand the message of God intelligibly. The situation has not changed greatly.

The Scriptures, which were written to tell the believer how to live a life pleasing to God, and were written in a language which the believer could understand, are the possession of all who desire them today. They were written in such a way that careful study will reap bountiful results. The child of God need not fear that he will err in understanding the Scripture because he lacks two thousand years of tradition to verify his interpretation. He need only know the content of the entire Word of God, and compare Scripture with Scripture to determine that his own interpretation is authoritative!

According to the documents of the Council of Trent and the Documents of Vatican II, the Scriptures are the authority of the Roman church. The term "Scripture" includes books which were foreign to the understanding of the term "Scripture" in Christ's day. The interpretation of all those books is a settled matter, based on the authority of the church fathers. This position is a far cry from the position which holds that the Word of God is sufficient for all of man's needs, and that the Word was given to men for their own understanding and study.

At the outset, the Roman Catholic church has demonstrated that their authority derives from the Word of God and other items of equal authority. Doctrine which is built on this foundation will only be as Biblical as those "other items" will allow. A system where the Bible is not the only and final authority runs a grave risk of building doctrine on a foundation not constructed by God.

---

1. General Association of Regular Baptist Chuches, "Constitution and Articles of Faith of the General Association of Regular Baptist Churches" (Des Plaines, Illinois: Regular Baptist Press, n.d.), p. 5.

2. Martin Chemnitz, *Examination of the Council of Trent,* Vol. I translated by Fred Kramer (St. Louis: Corcordia Publishing House, 1978), p. 37.

3. Ibid.

4. Walter M. Abbott, ed., *The Documents of Vatican II* (n.p., The America Press, 1966), pp. 118–119.

5. Chemnitz, Vol. I, p. 37.

6. Ibid., p. 38.

2/ *The Eucharist and the Mass*

James R. Lytle

The Elements of the Eucharist

Undoubtedly, the greatest area of difference between the Roman Catholic and the Baptist lies in the area of the celebration of the Mass. Too often, more heat than light has resulted from the consideration of this topic. This chapter will simply survey the approved Roman Catholic teachings on the matter of the Mass, and compare them with Scripture.

In reading a variety of Catholic authors, one will find that the terms "Mass" and "Eucharist" are occasionally used synonymously. For the purposes of this work, the distinction is important. Strictly, the Eucharist is the more narrow of the two terms. It may refer to only the elements of the bread and wine, or it may refer to the whole process of the offering of the elements. The term "Mass" refers to the liturgical service which surrounds the actual offering of the Eucharist. The doctrine of transubstantiation is related to the Mass.

The role of Christ in the Lord's Supper is understood by many in Christendom with many variations. In the view of most, there are two extremes in understanding the Eucharist. On the one hand, the Roman Catholic church teaches the actual physical presence of Christ in the elements of the Lord's Table. On the opposite end of the spectrum, one finds those who teach that the supper is a simple memorial service of the death of Christ.

The Roman Catholic understanding of the presence of Christ in the elements of the Eucharist is not a doctrine which has apostolic foundation in the Church. The real beginning of the doctrine of transubstantiation lies in the Middle Ages. A ninth century monk named Paschasium Radbertus was the first person to clearly teach the doctrine of "transubstantiation." He did not use the term, but the view which Radbertus held would later be called by that name. Specifically, he taught that "substance of bread and wine is effectually changed into the body and blood of Christ . . . (that) nothing else in the Eucharist (remains) except the body and blood of Christ. . . though the figure of bread and wine remain."[1] Radbertus did not teach that the elements actually became the body and the blood; to the participant, the wine and bread appeared genuine. In reality, though, they were the flesh and blood of the Saviour. Support for his teaching came from John 5:54, "whoso eateth my flesh, and drinketh my blood, hath eternal life; and I will raise him up at the last day."[2]

One of Radbertus' contemporaries was a monk named Ratramnus; he opposed the teaching of transubstantiation. He used John 6 to support his views on the Eucharist, as had Radbertus. His interpretation of the section was based on John 6:63, where Christ makes plain that He was teaching in a figure. Ratramnus and the other opponents of Radbertus made use of the teachings of Augustine, who is among the most highly revered of the Catholic church fathers. Augustine made a difference between the "historical and eucharistic" body of Christ.[3] Church fathers in the years following took sides for and against the issue.

The issue was settled by the Fourth Lateran Council in 1215. The theory of transubstantiation was no longer a debatable issue, but church dogma. Schaff quotes the statement of the Council: "the body and blood of Christ are truly contained in the sacrament of the altar under the forms of bread and wine, the bread being transubstantiated into the body and the wine into the blood by divine power."[4] The doctrine was vigorously upheld and defended by a variety of writers until the final and authoritative word of the Council of Trent.

The Trentine statement on the Eucharist is plainly worded. It is founded on a firm conviction that the Eucharist was instituted by Christ and the apostles and is taught in the Scripture. It was established by Christ for a variety of reasons; among these reasons are several statements clearly supported by the Scripture:[5]

1. Remembrance of Christ's works;
2. Shows forth the death of Christ until He comes;

3. It demonstrates the firm conviction of the coming of Christ according to His promise.

However, the Council adds some teaching which cannot be supported from Scripture:[6]

1. The Eucharist is a source of "spiritual food for the soul, for by it souls are nourished and strengthened" (Matt. 26:26; John 6:58).

2. It is the means by which Christ pours out His love upon men.[7]

The teachings of 1 Corinthians 11:17–34 comprise the only Pauline passage regarding the Lord's Table and the use of the Lord's Table in the Church. The first three items above are visible in that passage. The latter two are not, and no Scripture support is available to sustain them.

The teaching of Trent on the presence of Christ in the elements and support for transubstantiation is also clearly stated:

> Christ is truly, really, substantially; contained in the sacrament of the Eucharist under the appearance of those sensible things (i.e., bread and wine). . . . Christ exists at the right hand of the Father, yet in other places sacramentally. Unable to be explained or understood, but believed by faith through illumination . . . This is the clearest teaching of the meaning of "this is my body and blood."[8]

These assertions are supported in the Documents of Trent by the following passages: Matthew 19:16; Luke 18:17; 1 Corinthians 11:24.[9]

According to the Documents of Trent, Christ taught transubstantiation at the Last Supper—that is, as He stood there, the bread in His hands was His actual body and the wine in the cup was His actual blood (Matt. 16:16–28, etc.). In later times, the act of consecration by the priest accomplished the same result as the words of Christ at the last Passover (Luke 22:19; John 6:48; 1 Cor. 11:24).[10] Since the elements have Christ present in them, they naturally command worship. Therefore, the Eucharist can be worshiped as God, for it contains Christ.

The scholastic teachings on the exact methodology of the transformation and implications of this doctrine for everyday life are legion. The supposed miracles and phenomenal events which accompanied the presence of Christ in the Eucharist are also numerous. They can be studied in any standard volume of church history. The crucial issue at hand for this work is the plain manner in which the doctrine of the changing of the elements of the Eucharist is taught in the most authoritative of Catholic dogma. There can be no doubt that the teaching of the Council of Trent was based on the views of Radbertus—in opposition to the teachings of Augustine. The official doctrine of the Roman Catholic church demands a miraculous change in the elements of the Eucharist. Though that change is not apparent to the eye, or to the other senses, the church teaches that it is nonetheless genuine.

The Documents of Vatican II make no change at all in the Roman Catholic understanding of the transformation of the elements into the body and blood of Christ. Instead, the sacramental nature of the Eucharist is confirmed and stated plainly. As the "source and apex of the entire work of preaching the gospel,"[11] the Eucharist has a high place in Catholic thought. It foments unity in the church,[12] and echoing the words of Aquinas, "links together all of the other sacraments, which are directed toward it."[13] Since the elements are changed into the body and blood of Christ,[14] those who partake of the Eucharist are strengthened to continue in the faith.[15] Through the participation in the sacrifice of the Eucharist elements in the Mass, the believer finds a course of "hope and strength"[16] for the vicissitudes of life.

The material cited does not present a large corpus of information on the Eucharist, but it does summarize the essential teaching of the church on the topic. It is important that the Roman Catholic's entire perspective on religious life is channeled through his understanding of the Eucharist. It not only strengthens him for life, but is a "sacrament of love, a bond of charity, . . . a paschal banquet in which Christ is consumed, the mind filled with grace, and a pledge of future glory is given to us."[17] To deny the Roman Catholic conception of this doctrine is striking at the very center of his practical living faith. Nonetheless, the teaching of the Scripture must prevail.

The passages cited in the Roman Catholic documents to prove the validity of transubstantiation included the accounts of the last Passover of Christ with His apostles, His discourse on the Bread of Life (John 6), and Paul's admonitions to the Corinthian believers.

In John 6:51, Christ makes the clear statement "I am the living bread which came down from heaven: if any man eat of this bread, he shall live for ever: and the bread that I will give is my flesh, which I will give for the life of the world."

To interpret this passage with the wooden literalism of the Catholic point of view forces one to ignore the figurative nature of the "I am" statements of the Gospel of John. Few would attempt to subvert the figurative nature of John 10:7, "I am the door of the sheep." Christ had no hinges; He did not open and close in the entrance to the sheepfold. In John 14:6, when Christ asserted "I am the way," no one would interpret His words to understand that He is the macadam surface upon which one walks to the gates of Glory. The figurative nature of the Johannine "I am" statements should be affirmed by all.

In the passage in question, Christ Himself interpreted the figure which He posed. The demonstration of the fact that He is the Bread which all men must eat came in the sacrifice of His body on the cross of Calvary for the sins of the world (John 6:51). This passage does not teach that cannibalizing the literal flesh of Christ has an efficacious value for the remission of sins. If it does, much reinterpretation of the book of John is needed!

The Last Supper passages and the 1 Corinthians 11 passage stand or fall on the same arguments. Both the content of the quotation and the events of the Gospels occurred prior to the offering of the Son of God upon the cross of Calvary. His blood had not yet been shed; His body had not yet been pierced. The elements which the apostles perceived at the supper were those things which they had become accustomed to eating during their entire lives—actual bread and wine. Since this instruction occurred prior to the event of the cross, the apostolic understanding of the meaning of the elements would have involved nothing more mysterious than representation. The elements represented the body and blood of Christ. The apostles were accustomed to the manner in which Christ taught and His frequent usage of analogy and other figures. Simple chronology negates the Roman interpretation of these passages.

The elements of the Eucharist were not intended to contain the body and blood of Christ. The bread and wine did not contain the body and blood in any literal sense at the last Passover, and the New Testament does not even allude to the fact that they contained the body and blood at a later date. At best, the teaching of the transubstantiation of the elements adds to Scripture that which is not contained therein—and clear meaning of some passages must be misunderstood to prove a doctrinal point. However, the greatest danger of the doctrine of transubstantiation is evident when one understands the relationship of the Eucharist to the Mass.

The Celebration of the Mass

The celebration of the Mass is based upon the dogma of the Council of Trent. It is a "true and proper sacrifice . . . a propitiatory service."[18] In the Mass, the Catholic believes that he has grace imparted to him through a "re-sacrifice" of the body of Jesus Christ by the work of the priest.[19] In the celebration of the Mass, the Eucharist is changed from bread and wine to body and blood, though it remains in the appearance of bread and wine to the eyes of those participating.

The dogmas of Trent teach that the Mass is much more than just a memorial. In the Passover which preceded His death, Christ "instituted a new Passover, Himself, to be sacrificed by the church through the priests, under visible signs, in remembrance of His passing out of this world . . ."[20] The Mass is based upon the concept that the sacrifice of Christ is repeated again and again. The purpose of the sacrifice of the Mass is contained in chapter two of the Trentine statement on the Mass:

> This sacrifice is truly propitiatory . . . placated by this One's sacrifice, the Lord, granting grace and the gift of penitence, forgives offenses and sins, even enormous ones. For the sacrificial victim is one and the same, the same now offering through the ministry of the priest who then offered himself on the cross, the manner of offering alone being different. The fruits of this offering (I speak of the bloody one) are exceedingly abundantly received through this unbloody one.[21]

The intention of the Council of Trent was to teach that the offering of the sacrifice of the Mass was identical in effect to the offering of Christ on the cross of Calvary, though it differed in process of offering. Certainly, an immediate charge which might be laid against such a theory is that it detracts from the effect of the cross—as if Christ's death were not sufficient for the forgiveness of sin. In anticipation of this charge, the Council of Trent stated, "There is no chance at all that anything would be detracted from the former by the latter."[22] In context, the former refers to the work of Christ on Calvary, the latter refers to the work of the priest in offering the Mass. The church authority for making such a statement is "according to the traditions of the apostles."[23] Again, the issue of authority surfaces. The question is left begging an answer, based on the supposed authority of the apostles.

The basis for the Roman Catholic doctrine of the sacrifice of the Mass is the Old Testament system of sacrifices. Rather than continue to offer sacrifices of animals on altars, the church stated that Christ instituted a single new victim for sacrifice—Himself. This victim is offered again and again on altars in the stead of animal sacrifices. The Old Testament "economy" prevails unchanged, and the sacrifices continue; only the victim is changed.

In the canons accompanying the teaching on the Mass, the church makes clear that opposition to this doctine is not allowed. Specifically, those who do not recognize "that Christ is given us to eat"[24] are accursed. In addition, the last Passover of Christ "constituted" the apostles as priests, and "ordained" that they should offer the sacrifice of His body.[25] Those who fail to recognize this fact are similarly accursed.

In the previous quotation from the Council of Trent, it is stated that the church does recognize the Mass as a memorial, but the Canons of Trent will not limit its significance to a mere memorial service. "If anyone says that the Mass is merely a sacrifice of praise and thanksgiving or a bare commemoration of the sacrifice . . . let him be anathema."[26]

The Mass is also beneficial to those who are dead! Its offering affords forgiveness of the "sins, punishments, satisfactions, and other necessities of the faithful who are living, but also for those who have died in Christ and have not yet been fully purified."[27] The Mass, according to the Council of Trent, can take away the sins of those who are departed from this life, and even effect the purification of those who died in their sins.

The teachings of Trent are not devoid of the realization that Christ actually died only once, in spite of the seeming contradiction of the Mass. In fact the word "once" occurs twice in the early part of the constitution on the Mass:

> . . . He was about to offer himself once on the altar of the cross of God the Father through his intervening death in order that he might work out an everlasting redemption, nevertheless, because his priesthood was not to be ended through his death, in order to leave to his beloved bride, the

Church, in His last supper, which he gave in the night in which he was betrayed, a visible sacrifice (such as human nature requires) by which that bloody sacrifice once to be performed on the cross to be represented, its memory remain to the end of the world, and its salutary power applied for the remission of the sins we daily commit . . . offered up His body and blood under the species of bread and wine to the Father.[28]

The Council of Trent teaches that the cross work of Christ only occurred one time, but that the saving work of Christ occurs many times, based upon the work on the cross. In fact, Christ Himself offered His body at the last Passover before He ever offered His body on the cross. The last Passover, if interpreted to signify transubstantiation, was a sacrifice of Christ prior to the sacrifice of Calvary!

The Mass has the effect of aiding man to remember, according to the quotation above. Because of human nature, the church requires something visible to recall the sacrifice of Christ, lest they allow it to slip away from memory. In participating in the sacrifice of the Mass, Trentine theology desires the recollection of the continuing priestly ministry of Christ for the believer. Thus, the Mass is both a memorial service and a sacramental sacrifice of Christ for current sins of the living and past sins of the dead.

Vatican II did not alter the dogma of Trent, but did seek for more laity participation in the liturgy in general. The Mass is still viewed as the center of church life. It is a sacrifice in which Christ is actually present, and the communicant receives the actual body and blood of Christ in the form of the elements.[29]

In order to effect changes to make the Mass more understandable to the laity, the Vatican II documents call for the revision of the Mass

in such a way that the intrinsic nature and purpose of its several parts . . . can be more clearly manifested, and that devout and active participation by the faithful can be more easily accomplished.[30]

This would be accomplished by the simplification of the rite, and the deletion of things "added with little advantage"[31] over the course of time. Vatican II allows the addition of some rites to the Mass, if they will serve to make it more understandable. One important qualification exists for any such additions: each must be an addition "which has suffered injury through accidents of history . . . restored to the earlier norm of the holy fathers."[32] Actually, anything new added to the Mass will not be viewed as "new" in the perspective of the church. They will only be those things which were done by the fathers but lost during the passage of time. There is no change for the sake of change.

In a clear statement of harmony with Trent, Vatican II allowed participation by the laity in both of the elements. Trent stated that only the bread would be offered to the laity; the cup would be reserved for the priest.[33] The Council of Trent stated that this practice of communing in "one kind" came into existence as the church exercised God-given authority; though Christ had commanded both of the elements at the last Passover, the church had determined that all of Christ was received in the reception of the bread.[34] The communion under one kind was to be considered "a law which it is not permitted to condemn or change at a will without authority of the church."[35]

In calling for limited participation in "two kinds," the Vatican II Council was careful to state their conformity to Trent: "The dogmatic principles which were laid down by the Council of Trent remaining intact, communion under both kinds may be granted when the bishops see fit . . . also the laity."[36] The bishop's authority to determine "fitting situations" was limited to private determination by the pope.

Thus, in the doctrine of the Mass, the framers of Vatican II were careful not to change the teachings of the Council of Trent. The only changes made, in careful accord with the teachings of Trent, allowed for more lay participation in the same sacrament which had been affirmed for hundreds of years.

> As often as the sacrifice of the cross in which Christ, our passover, has been sacrificed (1 Cor. 5:7) is celebrated on the altar, the work of our redemption is carried on. At the same time, in the sacrament of the Eurcharistic bread, the unity of all believers who form one body in Christ (cf. 1 Cor. 10:17) is both expressed and brought about.[37]

Conclusion

The issue of authority is a crucial one in understanding the teachings of the Roman Catholic church on the Mass. The interpretation of the New Testament passages has been established by the Council of Trent, as has been documented above. Teaching is affirmed by the Second Vatican Council. As long as the church is the final base of authority, the teaching of the Mass by the Roman Catholic church must prevail.

The church councils are not the final authority, though. As stated above, the Word of God claims to be all that authority in the area of doctrine which is necessary for the believer in Jesus Christ (2 Tim. 3:16 and 17). What is the teaching of the Word of God on this matter?

In the Documents of Trent, we have noted that the church recognized that the sacrifice of Calvary occurred only one time in history, but they teach that the priest offers Christ up again in the Mass for the remission of sins. The pattern for this continuing offering is the Old Testament Levitical sacrifice system. Where the Catholic church teaches a unity between the Levitical system and the practices of Christianity, the book of Hebrews teaches a distinction.

Hebrews 10:1 states that the law had "a shadow" of Christ, and illustrates the similarity between the sacrificial system of the Old Testament and the sacrifice of Christ. The writer of Hebrews asserts that the continuing nature of the Old Testament sacrificial system was a reflection of its insufficiency. Levitical sacrifices were not offered continually as an aid to the memory of man, but instead because "it is not possible that the blood of bulls and of goats should take away sins" (Heb. 10:4).

In most vivid contrast to the Levitical sacrifice, Christ ". . . taketh away the first, that he may establish the second. By the which will we are sanctified through the offering of the body of Jesus Christ once for all . . . For by one offering he hath perfected for ever them that are sanctified" (Heb. 10:9, 10, 14). Indeed, "if we sin willfully after that we have received the knowledge of the truth, there remaineth no more sacrifice for sins" (Heb. 10:16).

The teaching of the Word of God is most plain. When the one sacrifice of Jesus Christ took place on the cross of Calvary all the sacrifice necessary took place at that time. No further sacrifice is necessary because of the overwhelming sufficiency of the one sacrifice. The continual "re-sacrificing" of Christ in the Mass denies the power and efficacy of the work at Calvary. In addition, the application of that continuing sacrifice to those who have departed this life denies the teaching of Hebrews 9:26–28. As men die once and receive judgment after they die, so Christ died once to bear the sins of many. If the dead are not judged, but may receive grace through the sacrifice of Christ, then Christ must die again and again to supply grace. This cannot be allowed from the plain sense of Hebrews 9:28.

The Roman Catholic who participates in the Mass does not intentionally make light of the work of Christ on the cross of Calvary—but that is exactly the effect. In the highest expression of Catholic orthodoxy is entrenched the grave error of the continual sacrifice of Christ. The believer, who is saved by the sacrifice of Christ's body once at Calvary, has the responsibility of showing the Catholic his error in this crucial area. The work of God is done—we need no continuing sacrifice. Instead, God calls us to have faith in that one sacrifice and to wholeheartedly trust upon that one work and its sufficiency to deliver our souls from the hell that we deserve.

The Roman Catholic needs to know that it was "Neither by the blood of goats and calves, but by his own blood he entered in once into the holy place, having obtained eternal redemption for us" (Heb. 9:12). Christ is not present in the elements of the Eucharist, and He is not sacrificed in the Mass. His work and redemption were completed in the sacrifice on Calvary.

The believer must devote himself to the remembrance of the death of Christ. The true meaning of the Lord's Table cannot lie in any resacrifice of Christ, but in careful consideration of the working of Christ which has already been completed on our behalf. "For as often as ye eat this bread, and drink this cup, ye do shew the Lord's death till he come" (1 Cor. 11:26).

The Roman Catholic who participates in the Mass must understand that in the Mass he affirms that which the Scripture denies, and places hope for remission of his sins in the faulty area of man's affirmations. The Roman Catholic must realize that there is not a shred of grace in the Mass. Eternal life is not in participation in the Mass; but by faith in Christ, "Being justified freely by his grace through the redemption that is in Christ Jesus: whom God had set forth to be a propitiation through faith in his blood, to declare his righteousness for the remission of sins that are past . . . Therefore we conclude that a man is justified by faith without the deeds of the law" (Rom. 3:24–28). Conformity to the Old Testament sacrificial pattern through the Mass does not cause salvation; only faith in the shed blood of Christ will redeem a lost soul from eternity in hell.

---

1. Philip Schaff, *History of the Christian Church,* Vol. IV (Grand Rapids: Wm. B. Eerdmans, 1910), p. 547.

2. Ibid., p. 548.

3. Ibid., p. 549.

4. Philip Schaff, *History of the Christian Church,* Vol. V (Grand Rapids: Wm. B. Eerdmans, 1910), p. 714.

5. Rev. H. J. Schroeder, *Canons and Decrees of the Council of Trent* (London: B. Herder Book Co. 1941), p. 72.

6. Ibid., p. 72–74.

7. Ibid., p. 74.

8. Ibid., p. 73.

9. Ibid.

10. Ibid., p. 75

11. Abbott, *Documents*, p. 542.

12. Ibid., p. 343.

13. Ibid., p. 541.

14. Ibid., p. 236.

15. Ibid., p. 28.

16. Ibid., p. 236.

17. Ibid., p. 154.

18. Ibid.

19. Ibid.

20. Chemnitz, p. 439.

21. Ibid., p. 440.

22. Ibid.

23. Ibid.

24. Ibid.

25. Ibid.

26. Ibid.

27. Ibid.

28. Ibid., p. 439.

29. Abbott, p. 156.

30. Ibid., p. 155.

31. Ibid.

32. Ibid.

33. Chemnitz, Vol. II, p. 338.

34. Ibid.

35. Ibid.

36. Abbott, p. 156.

37. Ibid., p. 16.

3 / The Sacraments

James R. Lytle

The Sacraments

In the previous chapter, we studied the Roman sacrament of the Mass. For the purposes of this study, one sacrament was selected for more in-depth study than the other six because of its centrality to Catholic teaching. The purpose of this chapter is to lay a foundation for understanding the Roman perspective on the remainder of the sacraments. Though each of the sacraments will be discussed briefly, the thrust of the chapter will deal with the concept of sacraments in general. In accordance with the design of the work, only the most authoritative of Roman Catholic documents will serve as source materials for the study; however, the Bible will be the source of all conclusions.

The Concept of Sacraments in the Documents of Trent

The sacraments were the topic of the seventh session of the Council of Trent. They deemed it "proper to treat of the most holy sacraments of the Church, by which all true righteousness is either begun or if it has been begun, augmented, or recovered if it has been lost."[1] In other words, the sacraments are the crucial issue in the Christian life. They comprise the beginning, the middle and the end of the Christian experience. Even in the case of the one who might fall away, the sacraments provide the way of return to the fold. In understanding the teaching of Rome, the issue of the centrality of the sacraments is inescapable. For the Roman Catholic, Christianity can only be understood through the practice of the sacraments. According to the seventh session of the Council of Trent, the sacraments include baptism, confirmation, the eucharist, penance, extreme unction, ordination, and marriage.[2] The framers of the Documents of Trent wished to make clear that the issue of the sacraments was closed to discussion, even down to the number of the sacraments. Any person who said that there were more or less than seven, or who said that any of the seven mentioned were not sacraments, would be anathema.[3]

Lest we pass the term without definition, the Council of Trent (*March 3, 1547*) has defined the "sacramental" nature of the sacraments:

> If any one saith, that the sacraments of the New Law are not necessary unto salvation, but superfluous; and that without them, or without the desire thereof, men obtain of God, through faith alone grace of justification; though all are not necessary for every individual; let him be anathema.[4]

No plainer words could be written regarding the Roman estimation of the sacraments. They are necessary for salvation and they are opposed to justification through faith alone. By the teachings of the Council of Trent, it is plain that the doctrine of salvation by the grace of God through the faith of the individual (Eph. 2:8 and 9) is disallowed. Early in the proclamations of Trent regarding the sacraments is the limitation that the Catholic must seek the sacraments (or desire them) if he hopes for salvation. Simple faith is excluded, and the grace of God is imparted through the agency of the sacraments—not the agency of faith.

This evidences the "anti-reformation" spirit of the Council of Trent. The watchword of the contemporary Lutheran reformation was salvation by grace alone. No human work was necessary for the impartation of divine grace. Pure faith in the revealed plan of God for salvation was proclaimed by the reformers, and this was a threat to the Roman church. Those who receive the grace of God by faith in the shed blood of Jesus Christ on the cross of Calvary, who take Him as their Substitute and Savior, do not need the externalities of sacraments to impart or maintain grace. They have received the grace of salvation through their faith.

The documents of the Council of Trent (*March 3, 1547*) speak for themselves.

Canon V: If any one saith, that these sacraments were instituted for the sake of nourishing faith alone: let him be anathema.

Canon VI: If any one saith, that the sacraments of the New Law do not contain the grace which they signify; or, that they do not confer that grace on those who do not place an obstacle thereunto as though they were merely outward signs, of grace or justice received through faith . . . let him be anathema.[5]

The teachings of Trent limit the receipt of the grace of God to those who receive the sacraments. The grace arrives through the performance of the act of the sacrament (*ex opere operato*).[6] Not all Christians are qualified to perform these sacraments which impart the grace of salvation. Instead, a select group is empowered by the church to take the oversight of these matters. That group is the priesthood.

The Concept of Sacraments in Vatican II Documents

As has been observed above, the Documents of Vatican II make no changes in the essential theology of the Council of Trent. They do clarify the meaning of the Documents of Trent for the twentieth century Roman Catholic. Regarding the purpose of the sacraments in general, the Vatican II document offers the following:

The purpose of the sacraments is to sanctify men, to build up the body of Christ, and finally to give worship to God.

Thus, Vatican II offers a three-fold purpose for the observances of the sacraments. "They not only presuppose faith, but by words and objects they also nourish, strengthen, and express it."[7] One might have received the impression from the documents of the Council of Trent that the sacraments dispensed grace in a rather perfunctory way. Vatican II desires to make the sacraments a practical part of the life of the church member.

In the sentence which follows the one quoted above, the Vatican Council made clear the fact that the doctrinal position of the church had not changed: "They do indeed impart grace. . . ."[8] Thus, salvation for the Catholic person is locked into the reception of the sacraments. Whatever effect they may have on the life of the Roman Catholic is secondary to their initial and vital impartation of grace for eternal life.

The sacraments are not "islands unto themselves." Each one of them is designed to point toward the sacrifice of the Eucharist.[9] The Eucharist "contains the Church's entire spiritual wealth, that is, Christ

Himself. . . ."[10] This is not meant to demean any of the sacraments, but to indicate that the preeminence belongs only to the One. As such, it is "first among equals."

In the administration of the sacraments, the Vatican II document clarifies that which the Council of Trent stated regarding the role of the priest in the sacramental process. Specifically, the bishops need to recall that "they have been taken from among men and appointed their representatives before God in order to offer gifts and sacrifices for sins."[11] The sacraments are not effective unless they are administered with the supervision of the bishop—at least indirectly. The priest receives his authority only through the authority of the bishop over him.[12] The priest has the care of a certain part of the diocese under the direct supervision of the bishop.[13]

The priest, or pastor of the local Roman congregation, has the following responsibility to his flock:

> In discharging their duty to sanctify their people, pastors should arrange for the celebration of the Eucharistic Sacrifice to be the center and culmination of the whole life of the Christian community. They should labor to see that the faithful are nourished with spiritual food through the devout and frequent reception of the sacraments and through intelligent and active participation in the liturgy.[14]

It is clear that the authority of the priest must be central to the Catholic. The priest will determine the degree to which the people of any given diocese will be partaking of grace. Frequent reception of the sacraments is necessary to successful growth in the Christian life.

The teachings of Vatican II and the Council of Trent are essentially similar. In both, the Eucharist is the center of the work of the church. The other sacraments are essential and must be partaken of if the Catholic is to receive grace necessary to succeed in the spiritual life. The bishop, or the priest under him, becomes the central authority in local spiritual life, for he administers the sacraments and designs the sanctification of the people.

Though no change was made in the essential system of the sacraments, the Documents of Vatican II allow for some revision. This revision is not a matter of change of function, but merely change of form. A "substantial unity of the Roman rite"[15] must remain, but the possibility of minor adaptation for local needs was allowed by Vatican

II. The most dramatic of the changes involved approval for the vernacular celebration of the Mass.[16]

The Individual Sacraments

With the backdrop of the Roman Catholic teaching regarding the sacraments in general, we shall turn to a brief consideration of the six remaining sacraments. Since a chapter has been devoted to the Mass, no further mention of it need be made here. As always, the documents of the Catholic church provide the source material for understanding their terms.

Baptism

In Canon V on the sacraments in general, the Roman Catholic church declared on March 3, 1547 that the rite of baptism was necessary for salvation.[17] Though grace is imparted at baptism, it might be lost at a later time by the baptized person, if he refuses to believe.[18] Thus, baptism does not impart a "sure" grace. It is involved in the process of salvation because it provides the grace necessary for salvation, but that grace can be negated by later actions of the person. Mere baptism does not insure salvation from hell; actions later in life can affect an otherwise sure destiny.

Baptism is to be administered to infants; in this way they become "truly incorporated into the crucified and glorified Christ and reborn to a sharing of the divine life."[19] The rite of baptism is the beginning of the Christian life and should result in a "full profession of faith."[20] The Council of Trent, understanding that an infant cannot willfully appreciate the significance of baptism, offers no reason for the denial of the efficacy of the rite.[21]

Confirmation

Confirmation is the voluntary rite intended to logically follow that involuntary rite of infant baptism. In this sacrament, those who have been baptized demonstrate before others the validity of their "rebirth" experience. They must confess before men the faith "which they have received from God through the church."[22]

In addition to the public profession of that which was supposedly endowed by baptism, the sacrament of confirmation endows the participant with special strength from the Holy Spirit. With this strength, the Roman Catholic believers are "more strictly obliged to spread and defend the faith both by word and by deed as true witnesses of Christ."[23] In other words, those who are confirmed (and that should be all who are baptized) are to be active witnesses and apologists for the church. The sacrament of confirmation is, of course, obligatory. This is somewhat of a paradox, that the act which should naturally follow if the Roman Catholic doctrine of baptism is true must be commanded.

Penance

The Roman Catholic church freely admits that the regenerate do not always act as if they are regenerate. Since the Roman Catholic church teaches that the sacrament of baptism brings about salvation and regeneration, one might expect that the whole world would be running on a Biblical ethic. This is not the case, according to the Council of Trent, because man lacks gratitude for the regeneration received from his baptism.[24] The sacrament of penance will remit sins committed after baptism.

Penance was not a sacrament prior to the coming of Christ to the earth, and was committed by Him to the apostles for use after His departure to Heaven.[25] Both the apostles and their successors have the capability to offer full forgiveness to any who might sin after their baptism. The Roman Catholic church has used Matthew 16:19 to support their view that the church has the power to bind or remit sin. The opposing view that the passage is a mandate to preach the gospel, which truly frees from the bondage of sin, is anathematized by the Documents of Trent.[26]

The sacrament of penance consisted of four parts: There must be contrition or attrition (*i.e. sorrow over sin*), confession to the priest, satisfaction and absolution by the priest. Contrition involves both sorrow over sin committed and firm resolve to cease from the act of sin. The person who is genuinely penitent must actually have a hatred for sin.[27]

Confession is made to the priest because he has the power to remit sins. Since he cannot remit sins of which he has no knowledge, the Council of Trent requires that the penitent person speak to that one who has authority to loose his sin.

The power of absolution, or freeing from sins, was limited solely to the priests, and could be exercised by no others.[28] This so called "ministry of the keys" is an actual judicial act of judgment and justice. The forgiveness by the priest is the forgiveness by God. The priest is the vicar (*substitute*) for God in the matter of the loosing or binding of sins.

The matter of penance is a central issue to the spiritual life, according to the Documents of Vatican II. One of the directives to the bishops is in the matter of penance. If he desires to be a proper spiritual overseer to those in his diocese, he must see that the faithful take part in the Eucharist often, and this participation must be preceded by penance.

> Pastors should also be mindful of how much the sacrament of penance contributes to developing the Christian life and, therefore, should make themselves available to hear the confessions of the faithful.[29]

The Roman Catholic who is promised the remission of sins by his baptism at birth, must depend on the sacrament of penance to secure the eternality of his salvation.

Extreme Unction

This sacrament has been more fittingly cited by the Documents of Vatican II as "anointing of the sick." [30] It is a sacrament which brings penance to completion. The Documents of Trent offer James 5:14, 15 as support for the existence of the doctrine. The purpose of the act is explained as follows:

> For the things signified is the grace of the Holy Spirit, whose anointing takes away sins, if there are still any to be expiated, also the remnants of sins, raises up and strengthens the soul of the sick person by exciting in him a great confidence in divine mercy, supported by which the sick person both bears more easily the inconveniences and troubles of sickness and more readily resists the temptations of the devil, who lies in wait for his heel and sometimes regains the health of body when it is expedient for the health of his soul.[31]

In simple terms, the act of extreme unction is a preparation for death; if any sins have remained since the last penance of the individual, this sacrament will supposedly remove them.

As in the other sacraments mentioned, the anathema is applied to the person who fails to subscribe wholly to the precepts above. Included in the anathema are those who do not agree that the priests are the only ones who may administer the sacrament. If someone asserts that the "older men" of the given community are in the scope of the teaching of the James passage, he is accursed.[32]

Holy Orders

If the size of this work permitted, a chapter on the role of the priest in the Roman Catholic faith would be of great value. For the sake of the purpose of the work, however, the statements of the Council of Trent and Vatican II on the sacrament of Holy Orders and the priesthood will suffice.

The priesthood is logically the extension of the sacrificial system of the Mass, as the Council of Trent affirms.[33] If there is a sacrifice, there must be a priest to offer the sacrifice. Given the doctrine of the Eucharist, one must have the doctrine of the priesthood. The two stand or fall together. The visible priesthood is affirmed by the Documents of Trent (*July 15, 1563*).

> And the sacred writings show, and the tradition of the Catholic church has always taught, that this priesthood was instituted by the same Lord our Savior, and given to the apostles and their successors in the priesthood for consecrating, offering, and administering the body and blood and also for remitting and retaining sins.[34]

In this rather sweeping statement, the Roman Catholic church offers a job description for the priest. The priest will be a crucial element in the life of the Roman Catholic for the priest administers the essentials of salvation. These essentials, as stated above, include the Eucharist which dispenses the grace of continuing life in Christ and the remission and retention of sins which affects one's eternal destiny.

The "holy orders" is not a sacrament limited to the priesthood. Though no mention is made of six of them in the Vatican II documents, the Council of Trent lists a total of seven offices that function in the ministry of the church. In addition to the priest (*the highest of the offices*), the church also recognizes the function of the deacon, subdeacon, acolyte, exorcist, lector and doorkeeper.[35]

Of all the orders listed above, the office of priest is the most important for the Roman Catholic church. The priest is the one who holds the power of eternal life and death in the power of the keys; he also administers the Eucharist. In the Concilium series which followed the *Documents of Vatican II,* the crucial work of the priest is commented upon. In these current documents bearing the *nihil obstat* and *imprimatur* of orthodoxy is the following statement:

> The distinctive priestly role of ministerial consists in this fact: he has a two-sided relationship in the sacramental sacrifice. In the first place, he has a relationship with Christ. In the sacramental sacrifice, the ordained priest acts "in persona Christi." The real sacrificer is the risen Christ, who is no longer visible to the community.[36]

The priest is the embodiment of Christ in the sacrifice of the Eucharist. He is actually Christ present in body form! In confirmation of this fact, Pope Pius XII is quoted: "Christ is present as the sacrificer in the ordained priest, to whom he lends his tongue and hand."[37] The grace imparted through the sacrament of holy orders is a powerful one indeed, if it actually changes a priest into Christ!

Marriage

The last of the sacraments is that of matrimony. The Catholic church assigns marriage to the realm of sacrament because of the translation of Ephesians 5:32 in the Vulgate. In the English (*King James Version*), the verse reads: "This is a great mystery: but I speak concerning Christ and the church." The antecedent for "this" in the context is the relationship of marriage, and the responsibility of the husband to love the wife as Christ has loved the Church. In the entire passage, the loving and intimate relationship between Christ and His bride the Church provides the example for the relationship between the couple united in Christ.

In the Vulgate, the Latin translation of the Greek manuscripts, there exists a significant difference in understanding. The Greek word "musterion" (*mystery, above*) is translated by the Latin *sacramentum*. Thus, the marriage bond is a sacrament. Since "sacrament" by Catholic definition imparts grace, then marriage imparts grace. Latin does have the noun *mysterium* available to express something "secret" (*which is the meaning of the Greek term "musterion"*). The Latin translation of the word seems to add to the sense of the word in the intent of Paul.

It appears that the Vulgate translation of the term for mystery has added greatly to the meaning of the term. To be sure, the passage does teach the great sanctity of marriage by comparison to the relationship of Christ and the Church. This high analogy does not imply the application of the word "sacrament" though. The Roman Catholic church perceived correctly the high value that God places on the marriage relationship which He established, but they err in stating that it imparts grace.

A Response from the Word of God

The anathemas which are included in the presentation of the doctrines preceding should convince the reader that the Roman Catholic church is serious about their doctrine. These seven areas of sacrament form the core of Roman Catholic theology, and provide much instruction about the practical "living" of Roman Catholicism. It is necessary to examine both the concept of sacrament and the individual sacraments, using the Word of God as the standard.

The Concept of Sacraments is Unbiblical

The Roman Catholic doctrine of the sacraments is founded upon the concept of the cruciality of the sacraments. It has been stated above that the sacraments are the beginning, the middle and the end of the Roman Catholic experience. They cause one to enter faith; they sustain in the midst of faith; and they guard one from falling away from faith even at death. At least three reasons from Scripture can be marshalled to demonstrate that God has not bound His grace to external acts of sacraments.

First, instances of the giving of grace in the Scripture are not bound to externalities. In the instance of the Samaritan woman who met Jesus at the well, our Lord makes it abundantly clear that the location of her worship was not even remotely the issue. She had to have the correct perception of God—not merely the correct location for worship (John 4:5-45).

The woman of Samaria did not have to make a pilgrimage to a certain place, or do any other thing to receive grace from God. She had to understand the true nature of God and worship Him. Her response to the grace of God was evident in externalities. She immediately testified of the identity of Christ to others, and many Samaritans came to know their Messiah.

In similar fashion, the publican (*tax collector*) in Luke 18:9-14 demonstrates that externalities were not the source of imparted grace. If doing something could cause salvation, then certainly the Pharisee should have been redeemed! By his own testimony, the Pharisee was not an extortioner, unjust, adulterer or like a tax collector. He fasted twice every week and tithed all of his possessions. In contrast, the tax collector did nothing but pray to God for mercy, with the vivid realization that he was a lost sinner. In the words of Christ, "this man went down to his house justified." Justification did not result from something he did or from something done to him, but was derived from the attitude of the heart. The tax collector received justification without the sacramental system and without the offer of any Levitical sacrifice on his behalf.

Second, the Scripture demonstrates in a number of passages that the way of salvation is by grace through faith alone. One of the marvelous verses of the Bible is John 3:16: "For God so loved the world, that he gave his only begotten Son, that whosoever believeth in Him should not perish, but have everlasting life." In this text, the simple element of belief is the prerequisite for eternal life. No baptism is necessary to remove original sin, and no penance is necessary to maintain salvation. The believing one does not need extreme unction at death because from the moment of belief he possesses eternal life.

The simplicity of justification by faith is the theme for the epistle of Romans. In Romans 3:21–28, the apostle Paul argues for the sufficiency of faith as the sole means of receiving justification. Justification is "by faith of Jesus Christ unto all and upon all them that believe: . . . Being justified freely by his grace through the redemption that is in Christ Jesus:" (*vv. 22 and 24*). Eternal life and a righteous standing before God is secured through faith, not through some external means.

In the fourth chapter of Romans, Paul made it clear that his doctrine of justification by faith was not some "new idea" of his own making. Justification by faith is as old as Abraham—and older. Paul chose the example of Abraham's obedience to God in Genesis 15:6. God's subsequent declaration of Abraham's righteousness as the example of the antiquity of the doctrine of justification apart from any work was not the concoction of some obscure Reformation theologian. It is as old as the working of God with men.

In Titus 3:5 and 6, the Scripture teaches that God's mercy motivated Him to provide salvation for us. Our salvation is not by works of righteousness which we have done. Whether one interprets the "works of righteousness" as works which produce righteousness or works which are characterized by righteousness, the anti-sacramental meaning of the passage is unchanged. The issue at hand is that the work of man is in no way related to the provision of salvation by God. Man is responsible to turn to God in faith once he understands the facts of salvation by grace.

Finally, those things which are called sacraments by the Roman Catholic church—specifically baptism and the Lord's Table—are not sources of grace in the Scripture. This is certainly not meant to imply that they have no relationship to the life of the believer! They are a vital and necessary part, but not to the extent that they impart grace.

Baptism of Church believers occurred in the early hours of the formation of the Church in Acts 2. In Acts 2:38, Peter commands the concerned listeners to "Repent and be baptized every one of you in the name of Jesus Christ for the remission of sins, and ye shall receive the gift of the Holy Ghost." The preposition *eis,* translated "for" in the passage above, indicates the direction and the purpose of the baptism. The baptism is a demonstration of the repentant heart of the listener. The baptism becomes the proof of genuine repentance rather than the agent which causes the remission of sins.

Similarly, Acts 16:31 records Paul's command to the jailer at Philippi, to "believe on the Lord Jesus Christ." This faith, according to Paul, would result in the salvation of the jailer. After the exercise of faith, the jailer arranged for the Word of God to be preached to all the members of his house. Apparently their response to the gospel was similar to his, for both he and his household were baptized.

The pre-Christian baptism of John the Bapist did not effect regeneration. Instead, it demonstrated that the baptismal candidate was serious about his repentance, and was confessing his sins. No mention is made of the impartation of grace, but John certainly had some harsh words for those who failed to "Bring forth therefore fruits meet for repentance" (Matt. 3:8 ff.). John pointed out that his function was not to baptize in the same manner that Christ would baptize; John's baptism was only with water; Christ's would be with the Holy Ghost and with fire. This remarkable prophecy was fulfilled on the day of Pentecost (Acts 1:5; 2:1-6).

The simple truth of the matter is that baptism was never intended to introduce anyone to eternal life. Simple faith was the introduction to the realm of Christianity, and baptism was the outward sign of the reality of the inward profession. "For by grace are ye saved through faith; and that not of yourselves: it is the gift of God: Not of works, lest any man should boast" (Eph. 2:8 and 9).

In this example of baptism it is clear that the "sacrament" does not cause salvation, and that it does not confer any saving grace. The Roman Catholic doctrine that sacraments in general are designed to impart grace does not have the support of the plain words of Scripture. God teaches in His Word that eternal life springs from faith alone.

The Individual Sacraments

In the preceding paragraphs, the sacrament of baptism was presented as the response of the believer to the work of Christ in his life. In no instance does the Scripture allow for the baptism of the infant who cannot understand the significance of the action. In the case of the Philippian jailer, who was baptized with "his house," some have postulated that the wording "house" implies the baptism of infants. If such is the case, then the infants were baptized for a different reason than the jailer, who was baptized for his belief. The fact that the jailer determined to have the same word preached to his house as was preached to him in the jail should be an indication that a belief similar to his own preceded his household's baptism.

Confirmation is not mentioned in the Scriptures at all. The natural outflow of the Christian life should be a desire to defend the faith and spread the gospel. Instead, the Roman church teaches that confirmation produces these activities. In the Scripture, defense of the faith and spread of the gospel is required of the believer (Jude 3; Matt. 28:19). The believer is to live a life of witness, according to Acts 1:8. Witnessing is not only something a believer does, but something he is. The witness for Christ is to be a natural part of the Christian life. The Christian who does not witness for Christ is at best an abnormality, for he must deny with his life that which he professes with his lips.

Penance, as a sacrament necessary for the forgiveness of sins committed in the Christian life, fails to defeat the force of such passages as Hebrews 7:25 and 10:14. In the former passage, the believer is "saved to the uttermost" because Christ is interceding for him—not because he covers the sins of the Christian life with a penitential act. In the latter verse, the nature of Christ's sacrifice on the cross is such that by "one offering he hath perfected for ever them that are sanctified." Because of the work of Christ, God no longer remembers the sins and iniquities of the Christian. Where God has provided remission of sins in Christ, "there is no more offering for sin" (Heb. 10:18).

The act of penance in essence denies the sufficiency of the work of Christ. What He has accomplished on the cross does not need the support of any further action. When God saves a man, the Scripture gives no warrant for thinking that the salvation might be less than perfect or complete. In Romans 8:28–30, God indicates that He has a bird's-eye view of the salvation of any individual. In that passage the believer is informed that any and all events in his life are a part of God's purpose. They are beneficial to him and are designed to conform the believer to the image of Christ. In an overview of salvation, the believer finds that from God's foreknowledge of him to God's glorification of him, the whole of salvation is planned by God. It would be impossible to have the supposed grace of baptism lost in an instance of disobedience, even if the doctrine of sacramental grace were true. Salvation extends farther in time and eternity than just those few years of our lives here on earth. Those who are justified (*past tense*) are also already glorified in the eyes of God. There is no need for any action of grace to support or supersede the grace imparted by God at the point of the believer's conversion. As Jonah said in a different context, "Salvation is of the LORD" (Jonah 2:9).

The sacrament of penance does demand of the Roman Catholic a genuine contrition and confession. Absolution is then received from the priest. In the New Testament, contrition is not commanded but sorrow for sin is certainly implied in such a passage as 2 Corinthians 7:2–11. Sorrow over sin should naturally result from the proper perception of the nature of sin and the nature of God. The believer who realizes the penalty of sin and the price which God paid to redeem men from sin should be more conscious of sin than any other person.

The believer's consciousness of sin involves recognition of the improper nature of the act which he has committed. In 1 John 1:9, the believer is informed of the condition of forgiveness from God: "If we confess our sins." The word "confess" (*homologeo*), indicates that we have arrived at a point where we agree with God about the nature of our conduct. This "saying the same thing" as God would say about a sinful act presupposes a sorrow for the act. No believer who views sin as God views it could help but sorrow and desire a change.

The forgiveness provided by God is not something for which one must beg or plead. The confession is the only prerequisite to the forgiveness. The passage is silent concerning the need for a mediator to cause the remission of sins. The truth of God's forgiveness is so simple that some may stumble over it. Confession of sins—agreement with God that we have sinned—is the only prerequisite to forgiveness from our faithful God! No human mediator is judge over us; only our God determines the genuineness of our confessions. For the justified person, the forgiveness of God is assured because of the purpose of God in providing a complete salvation. His faithfulness determines that He will readily forgive the one who realizes the wrong of his action and who comes for forgiveness.

In the paragraph above on penance, the sufficiency of Christ's work on Calvary was suggested as proof of the impropriety of teaching the doctrine of penance. It is also the central issue in responding to extreme unction (*anointing of the sick*). There is no greater need for a special remission of sins at death than at any other time in the believer's life. The sacrifice of Christ on the cross, received by faith, has rendered void the need for further forgiveness and sacrifice. The one who is saved by God's grace is also kept by God's grace. The sufficiency of the work of Christ guarantees a full salvation and eternity with the Lord.

Holy orders, which impart grace to those who are to serve in the church, are most concerned with the role of the priest. As was stated above, the need for a priest is evident if the presence of a sacrifice is allowed. In no place in the New Testament is the Lord's Table referred to as a sacrifice of Christ (*see the section on the Mass and the Eucharist.*)

In fact, the only usage of the word "priest" in the New Testament either applies to the Old Testament servants in the temple, the believer in his prayer life or to the ministry of Jesus Christ Who is the great High Priest of His people. The word is not applied to the office of the bishop or to the function of the pastor or elder. In the Baptist church where these three offices are functioned in one person (Acts 20:17, 28; 1 Peter 5:1–3), the pastor is not a priest who offers sacrifice and prayer for the people. Christ has offered the necessary sacrifice, and each believer has the confidence of right-standing before God in prayer. Further, no New Testament evidence exists for the supposed impartation of grace through ordination. In 1 Timothy 3 and Titus 1, the qualifications for the office of bishop are delineated. Qualified persons do not need a special ceremony to infuse them with grace. Those who are qualified are to do the work, and expect success from the Lord.

That marriage is a great and holy estate cannot be contradicted (Heb. 13:4). The marriage relationship between a man and a woman was established by God at the time of creation. These facts do not warrant the assumption that a marriage ceremony imparts grace to the participants. The unfortunate Vulgate translation of Ephesians 5:32, mentioned before, will not stand the scrutiny of careful study. In short, there is no proof available for the impartation of grace at the time of marriage.

Conclusion

The Roman Catholic church has stated that the sacraments are a necessity for the impartation of grace to begin and sustain the Christian life. This has been established from the authoritative canons of the Council of Trent, and affirmed by the recent Documents of Vatican II. The Roman Catholic church has firmly positioned itself against justification by grace through faith alone.

In sharp distinction to the doctrines of the Roman Catholic church, the Word of God offers a free salvation to all who will by simple faith trust the gracious provision of God in Christ's sacrifice on the cross of Calvary. He willingly shed His blood on the cross so that "whosoever believeth might have everlasting life." He has placed no other conditions on man.

When Rome affirms the sacraments, it speaks against the very authority which it claims to uphold—that of the Word of God. The Roman Catholic doctrine of justification through the application of external sacraments cannot stand in the presence of the simple teachings of the Word of God. As always, the final issue is that of authority. Which one will be heard? Will it be the dictum of church councils or will it be the mandates of the Scripture? Certainly, we must place our trust in the infallible Word of God alone. Salvation is not by the acts of man but by faith, and faith alone, in the provision of God for salvation.

1. Chemnitz, Vol. II, p. 21.
2. Ibid.
3. Ibid.
4. Ibid., p. 61.
5. Ibid., p. 69.
6. Ibid., p. 81.
7. Abbott, p. 158.
8. Ibid.
9. Ibid.
10. Ibid., p. 541.
11. Ibid., p. 406.
12. Ibid.
13. Ibid.
14. Ibid., p. 418.
15. Ibid.
16. Ibid., p. 451.
17. Ibid., p. 450.
18. Chemnitz, Vol. II, p. 137.
19. Ibid., p. 143.
20. Abbott, p. 363.
21. Ibid., p. 364.
22. Chemnitz, Vol. II, p. 164.
23. Abbott, p. 28.
24. Ibid.
25. Chemnitz, Vol. II, p. 651.
26. Ibid.
27. Ibid., p. 552.
28. Ibid., p. 580.
29. Abbott, p. 418–419.
30. Ibid., p. 161.
31. Chemnitz, Vol. II, p. 653.
32. Ibid., p. 654.
33. Ibid., p. 667.
34. Ibid., p. 677.
35. Ibid., p. 682.
36. Edward Schillebeechx and Boniface Williams, eds., *The Sacraments in General, Concilium Vol. 31* (New York: Paulist Press, 1968), p. 99.
37. Ibid., p. 100.

4 / *Mary*
/ *Charles E. Jarvis*

Mary, the mother of the Lord Jesus Christ, is an integral part of Roman Catholic doctrine. All aspects of Roman Catholic life and worship are affected either directly or indirectly by Roman Catholic teaching regarding Mary.

Just exactly what is taught concerning Mary within Roman Catholicism is often hard to document. Nevertheless, it will be the purpose of this chapter to do just that, that is, document the specifics of the official Roman Catholic doctrine regarding Mary.

In order to arrive at official Roman Catholic doctrine we will examine the documents of the Council of Trent and Vatican II to see what they have to say about Mary. These documents are cited as containing official Roman Catholic doctrine by the hierarchy of the Roman Catholic church.

The documents of the Council of Trent make no direct attempt to deal with Roman Catholic doctrine concerning Mary. However, there are allusions to Mary which clearly indicate that the Roman Catholic church considers Mary to have been sinless. For instance, canon number twenty-three on justification in the documents of the Council of Trent reads as follows:

> If anyone says that a man once justified can sin no more nor lose grace, and that therefore he that falls and sins was never truly justified, or on the contrary, that he can during his whole life avoid all sins, even those that are venial, except by a special privilege from God, as the Church holds in regard to the Blessed Virgin, let him be anathema.[1]

The Blessed Virgin is a reference to Mary. It is the official position of the Roman Catholic church that Mary was the recipient of a special privilege from God which enabled her not to sin. Therefore, she is to be regarded as having been sinless while here on earth.

The Documents of Vatican II give a more thorough treatment of the official Roman Catholic doctrine on Mary. It is made clear from the beginning that the memory of the Virgin Mary must be venerated or reverenced in addition to upholding Christ as the Head of the church.[2] The Documents of Vatican II also point out that the sphere of authority for their position on Mary consists of a combination of the Holy Scriptures and these documents.[3] In essence, the various documents of Roman Catholicism are as equally authoritative as the Holy Scriptures. Therefore, it does not become absolutely necessary for all their teachings concerning Mary to be based only on Holy Scripture. Where the Scriptures do not address these matters, Roman Catholic documents do. The Vatican II documents go so far as to explain that if something they teach concerning Mary appears to contradict Holy Scripture, Roman Catholic documents take precedence and become the absolute authority for the basis of their teaching.[4] In a sense, Scripture is not even given equal authority with the documents.

With these factors in mind, we will now attempt to be as objective as possible and address Roman Catholic doctrine concerning Mary in three important areas. These areas are, Mary's role in salvation, Mary's standing before God, and Mary's relationship to the church. The Documents of Vatican II will be the main source of our examination since they offer the most thorough treatment of official Roman Catholic teaching regarding Mary. Finally, in each section we will take a close look at the inspired Word of God to see if Roman Catholic teaching regarding Mary lines up with the teaching of the Word of God.

Mary and Her Role in Salvation

The Testimony of Vatican II Documents

According to Roman Catholic teaching, Mary plays a very significant role in salvation. This is true by virtue of her very special relationship with Christ. This relationship is so special no other human has ever, or will ever, enjoy such a relationship with Christ. Roman Catholics are to "venerate" the Virgin Mary.[5] Veneration is the act whereby an individual is to be given special reverence and admiration because of a position of high achievement or nobility. In the end, it becomes actually a worship that is extended to Mary by Roman Catholics. Mary is to have this type of veneration or worship in addition to adhering to Jesus Christ as the Head of the church.[6] Both are equally important according to the Documents of Vatican II.

This very special place, which Mary is to be regarded as having, comes about by her consent to the angel Gabriel to be the Mother of Christ.[7] From that point on, Roman Catholic teaching is very explicit in maintaining that Mary was united to Christ, both in His earthly life and His Heavenly life thereafter. This unity is regarded as having been a close indissolvable tie.[8]

Because of Mary's consent to the message of the angel she is said to have given "Life to the World" and been endowed with the supreme office and dignity of being the Mother of the Son of God.[9] We would not deny that Mary was the physical mother of Christ. but Roman Catholic teaching intimates much more by that statement. Mary is given a degree of divinity as the Mother of God. Vatican II documents clearly state that by her office she "far surpasses all other creatures both in heaven and on earth." She is said to occupy a position that is second only to Christ.[10]

Further, by her consent or cooperation with God to be the mother of the Son of God, Mary becomes a bestower of spiritual life upon all the members of Christ.[11] She is clearly the mother of the members of Christ according to Vatican II documents, by virtue of the fact that she gives them life.[12] Mary, then, is united with Jesus Christ in the work of salvation.

This union with Christ in the work of salvation is to have been manifested from the time of Christ's conception till His death. When she visited Elizabeth, the fact that Elizabeth referred to her as "blessed" because of her belief in the promise of salvation and the fact that the baby leaped in her womb, is testimony of her close union with Christ (Luke 1:41–45).[13]

At the time of Christ's birth, Mary's joy in showing her firstborn to the shepherds and Magi is said to further indicate her close union with Christ.[14] Other references such as the presentation of Jesus in the temple and the events surrounding the time Christ remained behind to speak with the leaders in the temple are all said to indicate that Mary enjoyed a very special and close relationship with Christ.[15]

Aspects of Christ's public life and Mary's involvement are cited as well. In particular, the marriage feast of Cana is referred to. It is said that Mary was very instrumental in the beginnings of the miracles of Christ because it was by her intercession that Christ brought about the miracle of turning the water into wine which became the first of many miracles Christ was to perform while on this earth.[16] Mary is said to have received the praise of her Son during the course of His preaching because she was one who was faithfully hearing and keeping the Word of God (Mark 3:35; Luke 11:27–28; 2:19, 51).[17]

In relation to the death of Christ, Vatican II documents explicitly state that Mary suffered grievously with Christ according to the divine plan (John 19:25).[18] She is said to be united with the sacrifice of Christ by her suffering, willingly consenting to all these things throughout the course of the events surrounding Christ's death.[19] It is pointed out, as well, that Mary was present with the apostles prior to the day of Pentecost, praying and imploring the coming of the Holy Spirit by whom she had already been overshadowed. [20]

Finally, when Mary died she is said to have been taken up into Heaven in both body and soul.[21] There she was exalted by the Lord as Queen of all, a position which more closely describes her relationship with Christ the King of Kings.[22] All these factors and events are said to be testimony to the fact that Mary is closely united with Christ and, therefore, actively involved with Him in the work of salvation.

The role of Mary in salvation is said to be presented in the Old Testament as well as in the New Testament (Isa. 7:14; Micah 5:2, 3; Matt. 1:22, 23). The Vatican II documents state that her role in salvation was prophetically foreshadowed in Genesis 3:15.[23] She is said to be the Daughter of Sion which links her to key prophecy in the Old Testament concerning the nation of Israel.[24] Finally she is said to have fulfilled Old Testament prophecy by giving the Son of God a human nature.[25]

In an effort to be as objective as possible, it must be pointed out that in the Documents of Vatican II, Mary is said to be subordinate to Christ. But subordinate only in the sense of position as Christ is to God the Father. Roman Catholic teaching explicitly states that along with Christ she served the mystery of redemption.[26]

Futhermore, Mary is contrasted with Eve in much the same way that Christ is to Adam in these documents. As Eve was disobedient and therefore contributed to the death of men, so Mary by her obedience contributed to the life of men. As Eve was linked with the first Adam in bringing about the death of men so Mary is linked to the second Adam, Jesus Christ, in bringing about spiritual life to men.[27]

In summary then, the Documents of Vatican II clearly state that Mary plays a very important role in salvation. In fact, it is distinctly stated that she has the ability to impart eternal life and that through her we can actually partake of eternal salvation.[28]

The Testimony of Scripture

But what does Scripture have to say about these matters? For a fact, the Scriptures are in direct contradiction to official Roman Catholic teaching regarding Mary. Even though the writers of Vatican II documents make an attempt to harmonize their position with Scripture, the fact still remains that Scripture nowhere teaches that Mary can give life or save us from eternal damnation. On the contrary, Scripture very plainly tells us in Acts 4:12 that "Neither is there salvation in any other: for there is none other name under heaven given among men, whereby we must be saved." The context of Acts 4:12 is not discussing the Virgin Mary. Rather, the Lord Jesus Christ is the subject. Therefore, this verse plainly teaches that He is the only one Who can impart eternal life.

Furthermore, throughout the gospel accounts Jesus Christ repeatedly refers to Himself as the Resurrection. John 14:6 very clearly states that the Lord Jesus Christ is the Way, the Truth, and the Life. No man can come to the Father except by Him. There is absolutely no indication in Scripture that Jesus Christ shared His lifegiving ability with any other human, including Mary.

To say that Mary is actively involved in saving us from eternal damnation goes far beyond what the Scriptures say. A clear example of this is the teaching of the Documents of Vatican II that Mary actually suffered with Christ on the cross, experiencing the pain and anguish exactly as He did. Such statements have absolutely no basis in Scripture. Without a doubt, Mary did suffer a large degree of mental anguish as she stood there and watched her Son, whom she had given birth to and had raised from infancy, suffer the horrendous and terrible death of the cross. But it is absolutely absurd to suggest that she experienced exactly the same pain and suffering that the Lord Jesus Christ did. Scripture just does not say this. Such a position can only be based on human opinion and speculation.

Jesus Christ is the only Person we can look to for salvation according to the clear teaching of Scripture. Romans 6:23 says "For the wages of sin is death; but the gift of God is eternal life through Jesus Christ our Lord." The question simply becomes a matter of whether we accept the truth of Scripture or speculative human thought in regard to Mary. The answer to that question is quite obvious. As finite human beings we must accept the truth of Scripture because it is the Word of God. Even the hierarchy of the Roman Catholic church must admit this fact. No man is capable of knowing truth apart from the Word of God.

On the basis of the Word of God, the Virgin Mary plays no role whatsoever in salvation. It is by the Person of Jesus Christ that we are saved and enter into a relationship with God. "That if thou shalt confess with thy mouth the Lord Jesus, and shalt believe in thine heart that God hath raised Him from the dead, thou shalt be saved" (Rom. 10:9).

Mary and Her Standing Before God

The Testimony of Vatican II Documents

According to Roman Catholic teaching, Mary's standing before God far surpasses any human who has lived except for Jesus Christ.[29] She is said to be free from original sin. She was fashioned by the Holy Spirit into a kind of new substance and a new creature which resulted in her sinlessness.[30]

This sinlessness and holiness possessed by Mary began at the point of the conception of Christ. The fact that she was said to be "highly favored" in Luke 1:28 is supposed to indicate this. A good deal of emphasis is put upon the fact that Mary consented to the things which were told her by the angel before Christ's birth. This is said to further indicate that she was in full cooperation with God and thereby became the Blessed Virgin, Mother of God, holy and free from all stain of sin.[31]

She is said to have embraced God's will for her with a full heart and, as a result, devoted herself totally as the handmaid of the Lord to the person and work of Christ. All her actions thereafter were impeded by no sin.[32] Mary always did what was right and thought what was right. She became the perfect example of faith and charity to the people of God.[33]

She occupies a high office which was bestowed upon her by God. She is said to be the favorite daughter of God by virtue of her being the Mother of God.[34] Such an office places her not only in the realm of dignity but gives her some degree of divinity as well. She is said to be the temple of the Holy Spirit evidently possessing a special endowment of the Holy Spirit which no other human can possess.[35] All in all, her standing before God is one of supremacy and nobility. God made of her that which no other human could ever aspire to attain; sinlessness and supremacy.

The Testimony of Scripture

Examination of Scripture reveals a markedly different picture of the Virgin Mary from that of the Documents of Vatican II. Although the writers of Vatican II make an attempt to harmonize Scripture with their position on Mary, they fall far short of making an objective examination of Scripture in regard to the Virgin Mary's supposed sinlessess.

Luke 3:23–38 traces the genealogy of Mary. Beginning with the father of Mary, Heli, in verse 23 Luke follows the lineage of Mary all the way back to Adam in verse 38. Clearly, then, Mary is the offspring of Adam as is every other human. The significance of this fact is born out by an examination of Romans 5:12. This verse reveals that all humans, including the Virgin Mary, are sinners by virtue of their link with Adam. The only thing that remedies that sinful condition is faith in the Lord Jesus Christ Who paid the penalty for our sin by His shed blood on the cross of Calvary.

However, it is clear by our previous examination of Roman Catholic teaching concerning the Virgin Mary, as it is stipulated in the Documents of Vatican II, that qualities or characteristics are attributed to Mary which have absolutely no Scriptural basis. It is said that Mary, upon hearing the proclamation of the angel concerning the conception of the Son of God in her womb, believed and then because of her belief became a sinless human being. Scripture does tell us that Mary did believe the proclamation of the angel. But nowhere does it tell us that because of her belief she became sinless. Scripture also tells us that Mary did say that "Henceforth all generations shall call me blessed" (Luke 1:48). But the fact that she would be referred to as a blessed one in no way means she was sinless. Without a doubt, Mary was blessed of the Lord in that she was chosen to be the channel through which God in the person of the Lord Jesus Christ would become man. She was also blessed by God because of her faith and her willingness to be used of God to accomplish His divine purpose.

But the same is true of all children of God who are submissive to the will of God for their lives and willing to completely surrender their bodies and their very lives to God for the purpose of accomplishing His divine plan. There are many places in Scripture where men are declared to be blessed. This is always a result of their obedience to God in some area of their lives. But it in no way indicates that they are without sin.

The only conclusion that we can come to, based on Holy Scripture, is that Mary was no different than any other human. She was a sinner from the day she was born until the day she died because of her link to Adam. However, she did by faith enter into a relationship with God that resulted in her eternal salvation. The same can be true of any other man or woman who recognizes that they are sinners and puts their complete faith and trust in the Lord Jesus Christ Who paid the penalty for their sin by His death on the cross of Calvary. The assumption that Mary was sinless and had a very special place of nobility or standing before God is based entirely on speculation and human imagination. Because of this the Documents of Vatican II, which officially represent Roman Catholic teaching, fall short of even beginning to prove that the Virgin Mary was sinless. Holy Scripture absolutely nowhere presents the idea that Mary was without sin. It does not even slightly or indirectly indicate such a thing. Since Scripture therefore is our final authority on all matters, how can we then assume such an unbiblical position that the Virgin Mary was sinless. There is only one Person Who ever lived Who was sinless according to Scripture. That sinless human was the man Christ Jesus. God "made him to be sin for us, who knew no sin; that we might be made the righteousness of God in him" (2 Cor. 5:21).

Mary and Her Relationship to the Church

The Testimony of Vatican II Documents

According to Roman Catholic teaching, Mary now plays a very important and distinct role in regard to the church. As has already been mentioned, Mary has been exalted in Heaven by the Lord as the Queen of all.[36] In this high office, Mary continues to exercise her saving influences on mankind.[37] She has been united with her Son and with

His graces and offices.[38] As such she continues to win for us gifts of eternal salvation. She becomes a mother to us in the order of grace due to her saving ability and influences.[39]

It is stated that she is the one who fosters the union of the faithful with Jesus Christ.[40] She is the one who brings about the salvation of mankind.[41] However, the Documents of Vatican II are quick to point out that Mary's role in salvation in no way impedes the role of Christ in salvation. Rather they both work together and complement each other in the economy of God's divine plan of salvation.[42]

Mary is ascribed this lofty position and ability because she was united with the sufferings of Christ on the cross. In other words, she suffered with Christ in exactly the same manner in order to make provision for salvation. On this basis, then, she cooperated in the Savior's work of restoring supernatural life to souls.[43]

Mary also functions as a mediator between God and His people. It is acknowledged in Roman Catholic teaching that Christ is the only Mediator according to 1 Timothy 2:5 and 6. But Mary is worked into the picture by stating that she manifests or shows the power of Christ's mediation without diminishing it. In other words, she aids the mediation of Christ by making it known to the church. As a result, she, too, is considered a mediator. But it is distinctly stated that she does not interfere with Christ's mediatorial role. She cooperates with Christ in pleading the cases of those in the church to God the Father. In this role she is regarded as an advocate and stated to be such in the Documents of Vatican II.[44]

Mary is to be the object of preaching in the church. She is regarded as the one in whom is united the central truths of the faith. When Mary is preached, then, she summons us to her Son and His sacrifice. It is further stated that the church looks to her in order that Christ may be born and grow in our hearts.[45]

Not only is Mary the object of preaching for the purpose of bringing about salvation, she also functions as the supreme example and model for the faithful, or those who possess salvation, to follow. It is clearly stated that the church is continually seeking to become more like Mary and her exalted model of faith and charity.[46]

She is also the model or example for all those who wish to conquer sin because she herself conquered sin and became the ultimate example of Christian virtues. Mary continues to function as such without interruption until the eternal fulfillment of all the elect, that is, until the salvation of the elect is brought to its ultimate completion in glory.[47]

Because of all this, Mary is to be the object of complete and unrelenting devotion. She has been exalted by divine grace above all angels and mankind. Therefore, the church is to honor her with special reverence. It is stated that she reverences herself by her statement in Luke 1:48; blessed by succeeding generations. Therefore, the church is to honor her, giving her due reverence by liturgy or religious dialogue, giving special place to her images, and imitating her virtues.[48]

Mary also serves as the sign of hope, comfort, and protection for God's people as they make their journey through life on this earth. She is the one to whom the possessors of eternal life can run to obtain protection and comfort. She takes care of her own and in her the church has hope of salvation from the sinfulness of men and God's ultimate judgment on the sin of the world.[49]

The church is exhorted to pour out faith to Mary and to pray for her intercession in Heaven with her Son. She is the one who gives eternal life. She is the one who protects, guards, and comforts God's people. She is the one who helps the Christian to more closely adhere to Jesus Christ.[50]

The Testimony of Scripture

Not only do the Documents of Vatican II claim that Mary can save, but also claim that Mary plays a significant role in maintaining salvation. As has previously been shown, upon her death, Mary is supposed to have been taken to Heaven and given a position by which she cooperates with her Son, the Lord Jesus Christ, in influencing and affecting the lives of men and women on this earth.

The writers of the Documents of Vatican II are quick to point out that there is "one mediator between God and men, the man Christ Jesus," according to 1 Timothy 2:5. They even go to great lengths to try to avoid contradicting this truth of Scripture with their teaching that Mary mediates between God and men. But their efforts to avoid such a contradiction are futile and, in the end, they fail. Without a doubt, according to the Documents of Vatican II, the Virgin Mary is right now pleading our case to God as an advocate and a mediator. In essence, official Roman Catholic teaching ascribes to Mary functions which Scripture tells us only belong to the Lord Jesus Christ. As was the case in our previous discussions of Roman Catholic teaching concerning Mary, such a position has absolutely no basis in Scripture.

Our examination of the Documents of Vatican II also reveals other so-called characteristics and functions of Mary. For instance, Mary is said to be an encouragement and comfort to the child of God as he progresses through his earthly pilgrimage. But such a teaching is found nowhere in Scripture. The only source of the believer's comfort, encouragment and help in coping with the trials of life is the Lord Jesus Christ. Jesus Himself said "Come unto me, all ye that labour and are heavy laden, and I will give you rest. Take my yoke upon you, and learn of me; for I am meek and lowly in heart: and ye shall find rest unto your souls. For my yoke is easy, and my burden is light" (Matt. 11:28–30). There is no indication that Mary plays any role whatsoever in this matter.

Furthermore, the Documents of Vatican II stipulate that Mary is the hope of the church. Once again, such a statement can only be based on human reasoning, because it is nowhere found in Scripture. The hope of the Church is the Lord Jesus Christ and Him alone according to Scripture. Titus 2:13 very clearly states that the Church, which consists of all those who have put their faith and trust in Jesus Christ and Him alone, are "Looking for that blessed hope, and the glorious appearing of the great God and our Saviour Jesus Christ."

In conclusion, it is obvious from our examination of the Documents of Vatican II that Roman Catholic teaching consists of ascribing to Mary that which only belongs to the Lord Jesus Christ. Such teaching cannot be based on Holy Scripture because it is nowhere found in Holy Scripture. The Lord Jesus Christ and He alone is the source of the believer's comfort, encouragment and hope. He alone is the believer's Advocate and Mediator before the presence of God the Father. These facts are based only on Scripture and are not supported by the Documents of Vatican II. We must accept these facts as absolute truth. We must not go beyond the bounds of Scripture.

---

1. Schroeder, Rev. H. J. (O.P.), translator, *Canons and Decrees of the Council of Trent* (St. Louis, Mo.: B. Herder Book Co., 1941), p. 45.

2. Abbott, Walter M. (S.J.), general editor, *The Documents of Vatican II* (New York: Herder and Herder and Association Press, 1966), pp. 85, 86.

3. Ibid., p. 87.

4. Ibid., pp. 87, 95, 96.
5. Ibid., pp. 85, 86, 94, 95.
6. Ibid., pp. 85, 86.
7. Ibid., p. 88.
8. Ibid., pp. 86, 88, 89.
9. Ibid., pp. 86, 89.
10. Ibid., p. 86.
11. Ibid.
12. Ibid.
13. Ibid., p. 89.
14. Ibid.
15. Ibid.
16. Ibid.
17. Ibid.
18. Ibid., pp. 89, 90.
19. Ibid.
20. Ibid., p. 90.
21. Ibid.
22. Ibid.
23. Ibid., p. 87.
24. Ibid.
25. Ibid.
26. Ibid., p. 88.
27. Ibid.
28. Ibid., pp. 87–91.
29. Ibid., p. 86.
30. Ibid., p. 88.
31. Ibid.
32. Ibid.
33. Ibid., p. 92.
34. Ibid., p. 86.
35. Ibid.
36. Ibid., p. 90.
37. Ibid., pp. 90, 91.
38. Ibid., p. 92.
39. Ibid., p. 91.
40. Ibid.
41. Ibid., pp. 90, 91.
42. Ibid.
43. Ibid., pp. 89–92.
44. Ibid., pp. 90–92.
45. Ibid., p. 93.
46. Ibid.
47. Ibid.
48. Ibid., pp. 94, 95.
49. Ibid., pp. 95, 96.
50. Ibid.

5 / *Purgatory*

Charles E. Jarvis

The Roman Catholic Doctrine of Purgatory

The specifics of the Doctrine of Purgatory

In order to officially define the Roman Catholic doctrine of purgatory, we must once again examine those documents and books which are marked as containing official Roman Catholic teaching. Specifically, we will be looking at three such documents and books which treat this doctrine. The first two are documents which we have referred to previously in chapters one, two and three—the documents of the Council of Trent and the documents of the Second Vatican Council. In addition, we will examine a third official Roman Catholic source, *The Catholic Catechism* by John A. Hardon, S.J.

The documents of the Council of Trent: At the final meeting of the third session of the Council of Trent, in December, 1563, an official statement concerning purgatory was set forth. In essence, it stipulates that the existence of purgatory is a fact. The "sacred writings and the ancient tradition of the Fathers" are cited as the basis for such a proposal.[1]

It is further stated that purgatory is a place where souls are detained after they pass from this earthly life by physical death.[2] There they wait to be released to enter the glories of Heaven and realize full communion with God.

The release of these souls from purgatory is accomplished "by the suffrages of the faithful and chiefly by the acceptable sacrifice of the altar. . . ."[3] In other words, those still living on the earth are the ones who, by prayer and sacrifice, aid in bringing about the release of a departed soul from purgatory.

Furthermore, it is stated that the Roman Catholic teaching regarding purgatory is one of "sound doctrine." As such, it is to be diligently "believed and maintained by the faithful of Christ, and be everywhere taught and preached."[4] Also the bishops of the Roman Catholic church are to "see to it that the suffrages of the living, that is, the Sacrifice of the Mass, prayers, alms, and other works of piety which they have been accustomed to perform for the faithful departed, be piously and devoutly discharged in accordance with the laws of the Church. . . ."[5] Interestingly, though, no Scripture whatsoever is given to substantiate any of the statements in this document.

In other sections of the documents of the Council of Trent, some very strong statements are made concerning purgatory and those who reject Roman Catholic teaching concerning purgatory. For instance, canon number thirty concerning justification reads as follows:

> If anyone says that after the reception of the grace of justification the guilt is so remitted and the debt of eternal punishment so blotted out to every repentant sinner, that no debt of temporal punishment remains to be discharged either in this world or in purgatory before the gates of heaven can be opened, let him be anathema (be accursed).[6]

In other words, if you deny the fact that one must still bear the guilt of sin and continually do penance in this life and in purgatory after death even though he had been justified by grace, a curse has been placed upon you by the participants of the Council of Trent in 1547. According to Roman Catholics, purgatory is a place where certain individuals must go in order to fully pay the debt of punishment for their sins which they were unable to pay for while they were in this life. Only by the temporal punishment of purgatory can one who was faithless on earth hope to see the gates of Heaven open to him.

In the section of the documents of the Council of Trent which discuss the Mass, reference to purgatory is once again made. As has already been discussed, the Mass is regarded by Roman Catholics as the continual sacrifice of Christ for the sins of men. It is stated that the sacrifice of the Mass has two purposes. First of all, it is to be offered "for the sins, punishments, satisfactions and other necessities for the faithful who are living."[7] Secondly, however, the sacrifice of the Mass may also be offered "for those departed in Christ but not yet fully purified."[8] This place of purification is purgatory.

Later on in the canons, referring to the sacrifice of the Mass, this pointed statement is made. "If anyone says that the sacrifice of the Mass is . . . not to be offered for the living and the dead, for sins, punishments, satisfactions, and other necessities, let him be anathema (*be accursed*)."[9]

In conclusion then, the documents of the Council of Trent describe the doctrine of purgatory in this matter. First of all, it is supposedly a place where certain of the faithful in Christ go after death because they were unable to make complete payment for the sins in their earthly life. Once there they make payment for their sins by means of some sort of temporary punishment.

Secondly, their suffering in purgatory is greatly diminished and even terminated by the prayers and sacrifices made in their behalf by the faithful still living on this earth. Eventually, the gates of Heaven will be opened to all those in purgatory once they have made sufficient payment for their sins.

The documents of the Vatican II Council: Little is said in the Vatican II documents about the doctrine of purgatory. But what is said is quite significant. In regards to the faithful in purgatory who are still being purified, this statement is made:

This most sacred Synod accepts with great devotion the venerable faith of our ancestors regarding this vital fellowship with our brethren who are in heavenly glory or who are still being purified after death.[10]

Those "still being purified after death" obviously refers to those in purgatory. In essence the Synod or Council of Vatican II is reaffirming the traditional doctrines of the Roman Catholic church especially in regards to purgatory. In fact it is further stated that the Vatican II Council

proposes again the decrees of the Second Council of Nicea, the Council of Florence, and the Council of Trent. And at the same time, as part of its own pastoral solicitude, this Synod urges all concerned to work hard to prevent or correct any abuses, excesses, or defects which may have crept in here and there, and to restore all things to a more ample praise of Christ and of God.[11]

Very simply, the Vatican II Council documents merely reaffirmed the doctrines affirmed at the Council of Nicea, the Council of Florence, and the Council of Trent. They are to be maintained exactly as they were written in the respective documents of these councils. This obviously includes the doctrine of purgatory.

We have already looked at purgatory as it is discussed in the documents of the Council of Trent; therefore, we need only to say that the position of the Roman Catholic church on purgatory at the time of the Vatican II Council, which was held from October 1962 to December 1965, is exactly the same as it is presented in the documents of the Council of Trent.

The Catholic Catechism: We now want to examine a very important and recent book entitled *The Catholic Catechism*. This book, as do the documents of the Council of Trent and Vatican II, bears the Roman Catholic imprimature which marks it out as containing official Roman Catholic teaching.

In this book, John A. Hardon, S.J. attempts to delineate a contemporary catechism of the teachings of the Catholic church. Purgatory is one of the doctrines he addresses.

He first attempts to establish the basis for the doctrine of purgatory. He does so by appealing to the Scriptures and the tradition of the church fathers. As is the case with all Roman Catholic teaching, both Scripture and tradition are given equal authority as the basis for all doctrines.

The primary "scriptural" proof for the doctrine of purgatory is found in the apocryphal book of 2 Maccabees.[12] Initially, this presents an obvious problem due to the fact that, for the most part, evangelicals do not hold that any of the apocryphal books are inspired of God. Nevertheless, Roman Catholic proof for the doctrine of purgatory is rooted in the apocryphal account of Judas Maccabaeus' act of intercession on behalf of those who had died in battle. This intercession involved prayer and a purchased atonement sacrifice for these dead individuals. This historical event will be treated in more detail later on in this chapter.

The Roman Catholic doctrine of purgatory in the New Testament rests mainly on two passages, although others are cited. The first is Matthew 12:32 where Jesus Christ stated that anyone who blasphemes the Holy Spirit will not be forgiven of this sin either in this world or the world to come. Roman Catholics understand this to mean "that certain faults are pardoned in this life, and certain others in the life to come."[13] Those pardoned in the life to come are those who will be pardoned in purgatory as a result of the intercession of those faithful ones yet alive on the earth.

The other New Testament passage used by Roman Catholics to prove the doctrine of purgatory is 1 Corinthians 3:13, 15. In these verses, the apostle Paul states that "Every man's work shall be made manifest: for the day shall declare it, because it shall be revealed by fire; and the fire shall try every man's work of what sort it is . . . If any man's work shall be burned, he shall suffer loss: but he himself shall be saved; yet so as by fire." On the basis of this passage, Roman Catholics are quick to point out that the Corinthian Christians to whom Paul wrote believed in a purgation or purification after death by fire.[14] They also maintain that these Christians believed in the prospect of helping those in purgatory by prayer.[15] No Scripture reference is given for this except for 1 Corinthians 3:13, 15.

Hardon in his book *The Catholic Catechism,* which is endorsed by the Vicar General of the Archdiocese of New York making it official Roman Catholic teaching, goes so far as to say that "there should be no problem seeing in these passages of Scripture (Matt. 12:32; 1 Cor. 3:13, 15) a reflection of the common faith."[16] In other words the Roman Catholic church says that the Corinthian Christians clearly believed in a place called purgatory and actively offered prayers and sacrifice for those in purgatory just as the Roman Catholic church does today.

When it comes to stipulating the kind of pain or suffering one goes through in purgatory, the Roman Catholic church is less specific and dogmatic. To them purgatory is a real place. But exactly what is experienced by those who are there is debated by Roman Catholic theologians. In the *Catholic Catechism* it is stated that suffering in purgatory takes two forms. First of all, those in purgatory suffer because they desire to be with God but are not yet permitted to. Secondly, they suffer because they know that in life if they had only prayed more and done enough penance they would not have to be temporarily confined to such a place as purgatory.[17]

However, there are those in purgatory who suffer more extensively than previously mentioned. Their suffering includes the pain of sense as a result of the purging and purifying fire that is said to burn in purgatory. But, this too, is debated among Roman Catholic theologians.[18]

Purgatory is not all suffering, however. It is stated that those in purgatory also experience an "intense spiritual joy." This is due mainly to the fact that all those in purgatory are assured of their salvation. The

Catholic catechism goes so far as to say that those in purgatory "have faith, hope, and great charity. They know themselves to be in divine friendship, confirmed in grace, and no longer able to offend God."[19]

In conclusion, on the basis of the official documents we have examined, the Roman Catholic doctrine of purgatory may be stated as follows: Purgatory is the abode of those faithful in Christ who have died but failed to do enough penance for their sins while alive on earth. In purgatory, the inhabitants experience suffering and go through some sort of purification process most probably accomplished by fire. Their stay in purgatory can be shortened if those still living on the earth consistently offer prayers and sacrifices on their behalf. These sacrifices must be purchased. The more money spent the better the chances an individual's confinement in purgatory will be shortened.

Finally, all those in purgatory need not fear eternal punishment. Each is assured of ultimate release from purgatory into the glories of Heaven. Therefore, purgatory is viewed as not only a place of suffering but a place of joy as well.

The Effects of the Doctrine of Purgatory

Its effect on the Roman Catholic church: How does this doctrine affect the Roman Catholic church? Why is it so diligently maintained and encouraged throughout Roman Catholicism? The answer to these questions is quite simple.

First of all, the propagation of the doctrine of purgatory serves to greatly enhance the financial posture of the Roman Catholic church. Just as Judas Maccabaeus collected money for sacrifice for those who had died in battle, so today, sacrifices for the dead in purgatory are offered by priests only after they have received sums of money.

What loving relative and/or friend would not expend great sums of money to see that a dead loved one be relieved of his or her punishment in a place like purgatory. This is exactly what the Roman Catholic church emphasizes throughout the world. It is no wonder that the Roman Catholic church possesses such vast financial holdings and properties in various parts of the world. A large part of this is paid for by the monies received by the church in return for sacrifices made for the dead in purgatory.[20] It is easy to see, then, the positive effect the doctrine of purgatory has on the Roman Catholic church and why they so diligently uphold it and teach it.

In addition to the positive financial effect on the Roman Catholic church, the teaching of the doctrine of purgatory also serves to assure the faithfulness of vast numbers of Roman Catholic people to the demands of the church. Only through the priests may an individual purchase the sacrifices which are so desperately needed to release souls from purgatory. To turn your back on this fact would only assure the extended sufferings of loved ones in purgatory. So the people, in a sense, are at the mercy of the demands of the Roman Catholic church. They must remain faithful. Outside of the church they have no hope for themselves and, most assuredly, no hope for their loved ones in purgatory. Therefore, the Roman Catholic church benefits not only financially from the doctrine of purgaory, but also in numbers of people who embrace Roman Catholicism.

Its effect on the Roman Catholic people: The effect of the doctrine of purgatory on the Roman Catholic people is quite a different story. In contrast to the positive effect it has on the Roman Catholic church, the teaching concerning purgatory has a negative effect on the Roman Catholic people.

First of all, while monies paid for sacrifices to be offered for those in purgatory greatly benefit the church, they serve to increase financial pressures and burdens upon Roman Catholic people. As has already been stated, certainly no one who believes that purgatory really exists would spare the expense of seeing to it that their loved ones are released from this place of punishment regardless of their financial status. As a result, the poor only get poorer.

Furthermore, the rich maintain a substantial advantage over the poor. They can purchase more sacrifices and win the favor of more priests. This is extremely important since the priest is the one who determines exactly when enough sacrifices and prayers have been offered in order to release a person from purgatory. The only hope of the poor is to consistently give their lives and significant portions of their small incomes over the years to the church to the end that someday their efforts will be rewarded.

In addition, it is acceptable for a Roman Catholic to pay money to the church for sacrifices that will be offered after he or she dies. It is hoped that this will aid in securing a quick release from purgatory. Here again, the rich have an advantage. In the end, belief in the doctrine of purgatory only serves to burden the hearts and minds of the

Roman Catholic people. It bears no benefit except for the feeble and false hope that loved ones are being relieved of suffering and pain.

It is easy to see, then, why death can be a fearful thing for the Roman Catholics. They have no assurance for their loved ones or even for themselves that once they die they will immediately go to Heaven. The fearful cloud of the prospect of a place called purgatory always hovers over their heads. Funerals become events which invoke tremendous emotional and mental torment. Death offers no real hope, only the possibility of more intensive suffering!

No matter how you look at it, the teaching concerning purgatory negatively affects the Roman Catholic people. It places undue financial burdens on them and offers no real hope beyond the grave.

The History of the Doctrine of Purgatory

The doctrine of purgatory does not find its roots in the Holy Scriptures. Rather, the seeds of this doctrine find their roots in pagan cultures and societies. Loraine Boettner suggests that a teaching very similiar to purgatory originated among the people of India and Persia five hundred to one thousand years before Christ.[21] Their teaching on the subject involved the belief that after death people had to go through a purification by fire.

In the fifth century B.C., approximately four hundred years before the birth of Christ, the Greek philosopher Plato made some statements on the immortality of the soul which are extremely similar to the doctrine of purgatory. For instance, here is one of his statements on the the subject:

> These things being so, as soon as the dead arrive at the region whither his demon carries each, in the first place those who have led an upright life and a holy life, and those who have lived otherwise are judged. And those who appear to have led a course of life between the two, . . . and when they are purified and have suffered the penalty of their iniquities, if any of them has committed such, they are absolved.[22]

Clearly, Plato proposed that at death all humans fall into three catagories. The first consists of those who have lived an upright and holy life. The second are those who have lived otherwise, that is, wretched and impure lives. The third category consists of those who "have led a course of life between the two," that is between a holy life an an impure life. These go to a place called Acheron, according to Plato, where they are purified and suffer the penalty of their iniquities. Once this has been done they are absolved. Without a doubt, this third category of Plato's is the forerunner of the doctrine of purgatory. The similarity is much too close to overlook.

As we move closer in history to the birth of Christ, we encounter the apocryphal books of 1 and 2 Maccabees which are dated at approximately 150 B.C.[23]—124 B.C.[24] Here again we find teaching closely paralleled to the Roman Catholic doctrine of purgatory. In fact, this forms part of their Scriptural basis for the doctrine since Roman Catholics accept 1 and 2 Maccabees as inspired works.[25]

Judas Maccabaeus was a leader of the Jews in the Intertestamental Period during the second century B.C. He led the Jews in battle against the Syrians to prevent them from successfully assuming dominance over the Jews. At the completion of one particular battle, Judas was overseeing the gathering up of the bodies of Jews who had been killed in the battle. Much to Judas' dismay, around the neck of each of the bodies was found amulets of the idols of Jamnia. This was outrageous sin upon the part of these Jews for they were strictly forbidden to wear such items. Judas concluded that God had judged them by death because of their grievous sin. As a result, Judas found it necessary to make atonement for these already dead and departed Jews.

The book of 2 Maccabees records what took place.

All then blessed the ways of the Lord, the just judge who brings hidden things to light, and gave themselves to prayer, begging that the sin committed be fully blotted out. Next, the valiant Judas urged the people to keep themselves free from all sin, having seen with their own eyes the effect of the sin of those who had fallen. After this he took a collection from them individually, amounting to nearly two thousand drachmae, and sent it to Jerusalem to have a sacrifice for sin offered, an altogether fine and noble action, in which he took full account of the resurrection. For if he had not expected the fallen to rise again it would have been superfluous and foolish to pray for the dead. Where as if he had in view the splendid recompense for those who make a pious end, and thought was holy and devout. This is why he had this atonement sacrifice offered for the dead, so that they might be released from their sin (2 Maccabees 12:41–45).[26]

The parallel between this passage in 2 Maccabees and the Roman Catholic doctrine of purgatory is quote obvious. Those who died in that battle were judged to be sinners because of the amulets that were found on them. But all hope was not lost for these dead men because Judas and other living Jews took it upon themselves to pray for these dead men and have an atonement sacrifice made for them that was purchased with money. Clearly, they understood that these men were in an intermediate state somewhere in need of prayer and atonement on the part of the living in order for them to be forgiven their sin and enter into Heaven.

The exact same thing is true in regard to the Roman Catholic doctrine of purgatory. This intermediate state called purgatory is the place where the sinful departed dead go who were not guilty of sin worthy of punishment of hell. The means by which these departed dead are eventually released to Heaven are through the prayers and purchased sacrifices of the living faithful. Without a doubt, the actions of Judas Maccabaeus recorded in 2 Maccabees in regard to those who died in battle significantly influences and becomes another basis for the Roman Catholic doctrine of purgatory.

As we move into the second and third centuries after Christ, we encounter the teachings of the early church fathers which imply and, in some cases, clearly delineate a doctrine quite parallel to the Roman Catholic doctrine of purgatory. In the case of Origen we find the following statement:

> There is a resurrection of the dead, and there is a punishment, but not everlasting. For when the body is punished the soul is gradually purified, and so is restored to its ancient rank. For all wicked men, and for demons, too, punishment has an end, and both wicked men and demons shall be restored to their former rank.[27]

Origen taught that a purification of the soul was to take place after death. This purification was to be accomplished by fire.[28] Once it was completed both wicked men and wicked angels or demons would be restored to their former rank and favor with God. The parallel to the Roman Catholic doctrine of purgatory is quite obvious. This place of purification or purgatory serves as a second chance for all men and even angels. Once punishment for sin has reached its end, the doors of Heaven are opened and entrance is obtained. The only difference between the teachings of Origen and the doctrine of purgatory is the fact that Origen maintained that eventually all men and all angels would cease to be punished. Roman Catholics do not go this far. They maintain that there is a hell, a place of eternal punishment for the wicked. However, they clearly teach that purgatory serves as temporary punishment for those who are not so wicked but not yet worthy of Heaven.

In the fourth and fifth century A.D., Augustine, who is regarded by Roman Catholics as an authoritative church father, also propagated a doctrine very similar to purgatory. In his writings he made these comments:

> We read in the books of Maccabees that sacrifice is offered for the dead yet, even if it were read nowhere in the Old Testament, the authority of the universal church which clearly favors this practice is of great weight, where in the prayers of the priest which are poured forth to the Lord God at His altar the commemoration of the dead has its place.[29]

By this statement, Augustine concedes that the practice of the universal church in regard to sacrifices offered for the dead carries significant authority in comparison to the Scriptures. So much so, says Augustine, that such "commemoration of the dead has its place." But it must be noted, as well, that Augustine conceded that such teaching can be "read nowhere in the Old Testament."

Furthermore, Augustine makes these statements:

> . . . we should not think that any aid comes to the dead for whom we are providing care, except what we solemnly pray for in their behalf at the altars, either by sacrifices of prayers or of alms. Even this does not benefit all for whom it is done, but only those who while they lived made preparation that they might so be aided.[30]

Clearly, Augustine believe intercession for the dead could be accomplished by the living through sacrifices, monies and prayers. It is no wonder that the Roman Catholic church places its imprimatur upon these particular writings of Augustine since they serve to substantiate its teaching on the subject of purgatory.

Gregory the Great, pope of the Roman Catholic church from 590 to 604 A.D., became the first pope to formalize the doctrine of purgatory. In the book *Dialogues,* Gregory tells of two Roman Catholic nuns who were given the order by the church to amend their speech or they would be excommunicated. But before such an order reached them they both died. It was concluded that they had gone to an intermediate place of the departed dead where it was not necessary for those still alive to make sacrifice for them. This was done at the hands of St. Benedict. As a result, the nuns were restored to communion with God.[31]

When Gregory was questioned about the incredibility of freeing souls from judgment by those still alive in corruptible flesh, he made these remarks:

> Wasn't he also still in the flesh who heard, "Whatever you bind on earth shall be bound in heaven, and whatever you loose on earth shall be loosed in heaven"? His function in binding and loosing has been taken over by those who govern the church in matters of faith and morals.[32]

Incredibly, Pope Gregory stipulated that the power of Jesus Christ on earth has now been transferred to the leadership of the Roman Catholic church. Consequently, despite being in a corrupt body, these leaders have the power and the authority to remove the dead from purgatory by their own acts of the will, sacrifice and prayers. Such a position is still acknowledged today by the Roman Catholic church.

In 1274 A.D. the Second Council of Lyons formulated, in writing, an official Roman Catholic position on the doctrine of purgatory. It reads as follows:

> If those who are truly repentant die in charity before they have done sufficient penance for their sins of omission and commission, their souls are cleansed after death in purgatorial or cleansing punishments.
> The suffrages of the faithful on earth can be of great help in relieving these punishments, as, for instance, the Sacrifice of the Mass, prayers, alms giving, and other religious deeds which, in the manner of the church, the faithful are accustomed to offer for others of the faithful.[33]

This statement was reaffirmed exactly as it is stated here at the Council of the Eastern Churches which was held in Florence some two hundred years later.[34] Further reaffirmations of the doctrine of purgatory were made at the Council of Trent in the sixteenth century A.D. and at the Second Vatican Council in this century. These were treated in more detail in the previous section of this chapter.

In conclusion, we must reemphasize as we did at the first, that the doctrine of purgatory has no basis in Holy Scripture. Instead it has been shown that its roots lie in the paganism of one such as Plato and then develops into a more specific doctrine as we progress through the history and tradition of the Roman Catholic church. The following question must be addressed at this point. Are history, tradition and the opinions of learned and highly esteemed men sufficient evidence to prove the existence of a place called purgatory? Or must we regard the Holy Scriptures, inspired of God, as the sole authority in determining if such a place really exists? Before answering this question, let's examine what the Holy Scriptures have to say about life after death and the possibility of a place like purgatory.

The Scripture and The Doctrine of Purgatory

As has been previously stated in this chapter, the Roman Catholic doctrine of purgatory has absolutely no adequate basis in Scripture. The Roman Catholics claim that it is Scriptural because of the account of the act of Judas Maccabaeus in the book of 2 Maccabees. But 2 Maccabees has never been accepted as an inspired book by the general populace of evangelicals from the time of the early church in the first century A.D. until the present.

The New Testament does not even hint of a place called purgatory although Roman Catholics insist that certain passages do indeed refer to purgatory. In addition to the two passages cited previously, other New Testament verses which they cite in an attempt to prove the doctrine of purgatory are as follows: ". . . he shall baptize you with the Holy Ghost and with fire" (Matt. 3:11). ". . . but whosoever speaketh against the Holy Ghost, it shall not be forgiven him, neither in this world, neither in the world to come" (Matt. 12:32). "If any man's work shall be burned, he shall suffer loss: but he himself shall be saved; yet so as by fire" (1 Cor. 3:15). "By which also he (*Christ*) went and preached unto the spirits in prison; which sometime were disobedient, when once the longsuffering of God waited in the days of Noah, while the ark was a preparing, wherein few, that is, eight souls were saved by water" (1 Pet. 3:19, 20). "And of some have compassion, making a difference: And others save with fear, pulling them out of the fire; hating even the garment spotted by the flesh" (Jude 22, 23).

A simple study of the context of these verses clearly shows that to suggest they speak of purgatory is absolutely unfitting to the context. It comes down to a clear case of taking Scripture out of context to make it mean what you want it to mean. Such a shoddy treatment of interpreting God's holy Word lacks clear contextual verification.

In order to show that the doctrine of purgatory lacks clear Scriptural support, one need only cite those passages of Scripture which deal with the death of Christ and the benefit it affords those who have trusted Him and Him alone for their salvation. Once an individual has accepted Christ as his or her Savior, the Bible tells us that the immediate result is eternal life. John 3:16, 5:24 and Romans 6:23 are just a few of these verses. The one who believes on Christ and His shed blood on the cross for his or her sin at that very moment possesses a life that is eternal. These need not fear detention in purgatory when they die, but can look forward with great anticipation to being immediately present with the Lord once having become absent from the body (1 Cor. 5:8).

Furthermore, those who have accepted Christ as their Savior stand completely justified before God the Father. They can no longer be condemned for their sin because Christ has suffered once the penalty for their sin on their behalf. John 3:18 tells us that "He that believeth on Him (*Jesus Christ*) is not condemned. . . ." Romans 8:1 tells us that "There is therefore now no condemnation to them which are in Christ Jesus." Since the believer can no longer be condemned for his or her sin, how can there possibly be such a place as purgatory where believers are said to undergo suffering and pain for their sin? The God Who promised eternal life and no condemnation to those who believe on His Son Jesus Christ would never subject the believer to such suffering and pain after death.

Another very important fact that the Roman Catholics fail to see is that the Scriptures plainly tell us that Christ has suffered *once* for sin. In the context of one of the passages they use to prove the doctrine of purgatory this statement is made: "For Christ also hath once suffered for sins, the just for the unjust, that he might bring us to God, being put to death in the flesh, but quickened by the Spirit" (1 Pet. 3:18). To say that the believer must continue to suffer for his sin even after he or she has died is to say that Christ's suffering and death on the cross was insufficient to accomplish payment for sin. Such would only lead one to conclude that Christ Himself was insufficient and, therefore, not God.

But the Scripture doesn't say that at all. Christ was God and as such made a full and complete payment for our sin once and for all. First John 1:7 states that "the blood of Jesus Christ His Son cleanseth us from all sin." Further, we read in verse 9 that "if we confess our sins, he is faithful and just to forgive us our sins." Along these same lines, the writer of the book of Hebrews makes this statement, "And their sins and iniquities will I remember no more" (Heb. 10:17). All this is made possible because of the sufficient sacrifice of Jesus Christ on the cross for our sin. Full forgiveness of sin, no condemnation and life eternal is ours if we "Believe on the Lord Jesus Christ" (Act. 16:31). There is absolutely no need for such a place as purgatory and, therefore, such a place Scripturally does not exist.

In summary, on the basis of the evidence that has been cited, we must conclude that purgatory is nothing more than a mythical place. The teaching regarding such a place finds its roots in paganism and not in the inspired Word of God. Christ has made a complete and final sacrifice for our sin by His death on the cross. There is no need for the believer to make further sacrifice for sin. To believe that a place called purgatory exists is to deny these very obvious truths of God's Word.

---

1. Schroeder, Rev. H. J., *Canons and Decrees of the Council of Trent* " (London: B. Herder Book Co., 1941), p. 214.

2. Ibid.

3. Ibid.

4. Ibid.

5. Ibid.

6. Ibid., p. 46.

7. Ibid., p. 146.

8. Ibid.

9. Ibid., p. 149.

10. Abbot, Walter M., general editor, *The Documents of Vatican II* (New York: Herder and Herder and Associated Press, 1966), pp. 83, 84.

11. Ibid., p. 84.

12. Hardon, John A., *The Catholic Catechism* (Garden City, New York: Doubleday & Company, Inc., 1973), pp. 275, 276.

13. Ibid., p. 276.

14. Ibid.

15. Ibid., pp. 276, 277.

16. Ibid., p. 277.

17. Ibid., pp. 278, 279.

18. Ibid., p. 279.

19. Ibid., pp. 279, 280.

20. "The Vatican: A Glimpse into the Papal Purse," *Business Week* (December 24, 1979). p. 52.

21. Boettner, Loraine, *Roman Catholicism* (Philadelphia: Presbyterian & Reformed Pub. Co., 1962), pp. 228, 229.

22. Plato, *Plato on the Immortality of the Soul* (New York: Hurst & Company Pub., 1956), pp. 109, 110.

23. Fairweather and Black, *The First Book of Maccabbees* (Cambridge: University Press, 1967), p. 43.

24. Bartlett, John R., *First and Second Books of the Maccabees* (New York, Cambridge University Press), p. 215.

25. Hardon, John A., *The Catholic Catechism* (Garden City, New York: Doubleday & Company, Inc.), p. 275.

26. Bartlett, John R., *First and Second Books of the Maccabees* (New York: Cambridge University Press), pp. 317, 318.

27. Origen, *On First Principles* (Gloucester, Mass.: Peter Smith), p. 146.

28. Ibid., p. 144.

29. Augustine, *Treatises on Marriage and Other Subjects* (New York: Fathers of the Church, Inc.), p. 353.

30. Ibid., p. 383.

31. Benedict, Saint, *The Dialogues of Gregory the Great* (New York: Bobbs-Merrill Company, Inc.), pp. 33, 34.

32. Ibid., p. 34.

33. Second Council of Lyons, "Profession of Faith of Michael Palaeologus:" Denzinger 464 (856).

34. Hardon, John A., *The Catholic Catechism* (Garden City, New York: Doubleday & Company, Inc.), p. 277.

6 / Roman Catholic Pentecostalism
Charles E. Jarvis

In recent years a new and significant development has occurred within the Roman Catholic church. Among Catholics in the United States it is commonly referred to as the "Charismatic Renewal." In general, it is referred to as "Catholic Pentecostalism" or "Catholic Neo-Pentecostalism." These terms or titles will be further discussed and defined as we move through the chapter.

However, before we can discuss Catholic Pentecostalism we must first of all discuss Pentecostalism in general. This is necessary because the Pentecostal movement originated and was in full bloom long before it cropped up within the Roman Catholic church.

The discussion of the background of Catholic Pentecostalism will involve reference to a book entitled *Catholic Pentecostalism* written by a French Catholic Theologian named Rene Laurentin. Laurentin is currently a professor at the Catholic University in Angers, France. Reference to this book will aid in making an objective assessment of the background of Catholic Pentecostalism.

The Background of Catholic Pentecostalism

A Brief Survey of Pentecostalism in General

Pentecostalism may be defined as that religious movement which emphasizes the baptism in and outpouring of the Holy Spirit. This baptism or outpouring is manifested by the outward display of certain charismatic or Spirit oriented gifts such as speaking in tongues, healings and prophesyings.[1]

The term "pentecostalism" is derived from Pentecost which is the term used to describe the events that are recorded in Acts 2. Pentecost was marked by the apostles being baptized by the Holy Spirit. The apostles present at the day of Pentecost as recorded in Acts 2, spoke in languages that were completely unknown to them. Nevertheless, they were genuine languages because they were recognized as languages of the foreign visitors who were present in Jerusalem at this time.

The present day Pentecostal movement maintains that the Holy Spirit has renewed this specific operation and currently is involved in baptizing certain individuals today. The expression of this Spirit Baptism is, once again, speaking in tongues and the exercising of certain other charismatic gifts.[2] Pentecostals further maintain that this baptism in the Holy Spirit is a repeated event in the life of certain individuals and also that it does not necessarily involve all Christians. Only those who avail themselves of such a ministry by the Holy Spirit are those who actually experience it.[3]

Pentecostalism is said to have begun on December 31, 1900. A woman by the name of Agnes Ozman experienced the baptism in the Holy Spirit and, consequently, spoke in tongues. She was a student at a Methodist Bible School in Topeka, Kansas at the time of her pentecostal experience.

It seems that Agnes Ozman and other of her fellow students became quite concerned about the lack of vibrancy among churches of their day in contrast to that of the early church. The next day, on January 1, 1901, Agnes requested that her pastor lay hands on her as they had in the early churches in order that she might receive the gift of the Spirit. Her pastor agreed to do so and Agnes then described her immediate experience "as though rivers of living water were proceeding from my inmost being." She then began to speak in tongues and claimed that the day following her pentecostal experience a Bohemian recognized the tongue in which she was speaking as his own. However, she was totally unable to understand it herself.[4]

Shortly, thereafter, other students of this quaint little Methodist Bible School were said to have had the same experience that Agnes Ozman had had. Eventually, Pentecostal churches were organized and the movement began to gain momentum.[5]

Not only were specific Pentecostal churches organized but the Pentecostal movement began to infiltrate already existing denominations. Today it is estimated that there are approximately two million

Pentecostals living in the United States thriving and operating within thirty-five different denominations.[6]

Their influence throughout the world increases with every passing day. At present, they are very much involved in dialogue with the World Council of Churches which is the spearhead of the ecumenical movement. Clearly, it would be a mistake to say that the Pentecostal movement is merely a passing fad. From all indications, it is here to stay.[7]

The Development of Roman Catholic Pentecostalism in Particular

The Pentecostal movement infiltrated the Roman Catholic church for the first time in January of 1967. A Roman Catholic by the name of Steve Clark from East Lansing, Michigan had just finished reading a book by David Wilkerson entitled *The Cross and the Switchblade*. The book is the story of a pastor who chose to leave the church he was pastoring to embark upon a ministry in the inner city of Brooklyn, New York. Toward the end of the book Mr. Wilkerson emphasized the importance and need of the power of the Holy Spirit to accomplish such a ministry.[8]

It was on this point that Steve Clark and other of his fellow Roman Catholics began to concentrate. During the next few weeks, discussions among this group were centered around the Holy Spirit and the charismatic gifts of the Holy Spirit. As the discussion progressed, another book entered into the picture entitled *They Speak in Other Tongues* by John Sherrill. This book suggested practical ways of achieving this kind of experience with the Holy Spirit.[9]

Consequently, some time later, two from this group of Roman Catholics attended a Pentecostal meeting at a local Episcopalian church. At the close of the meeting these two men, Ralph Keifer and Patrick Bourgeois, asked if they might receive the baptism of the Holy Spirit. Both were prayed over and received the laying on of hands. Ralph Keifer claimed to pray in tongues almost immediately. He said that "it was not a particularly soaring or spectacular thing . . . I felt a certain peace. . . ."[10]

What followed was somewhat of a flowering effect. Keifer was a lay professor at Duquesne University. Shortly after his experience he laid hands on two of his colleagues. They, too, had the same experience that Keifer had. About a month later students of the Duquesne University reportedly experienced the baptism of the Holy Spirit of which some were said to have spoken in tongues.[11]

Two weeks later at the University of Notre Dame, students were reported to have received the baptism of the Holy Spirit and the majority of these, as well, were said to have received the gift of speaking in tongues. In the next weeks and months Roman Catholic students, professors, and even priests reportedly received the baptism of the Holy Spirit. From these centers, especially the University of Notre Dame, Roman Catholic Pentecostalism spread like wildfire in just a few short years. Presently, the movement extends to virtually every Roman Catholic environ in the world. Such countries as Puerto Rico, France, Italy, Spain and Germany are just a few of those experiencing the rapid growth and development of Roman Catholic Pentecostalism.[12]

This movement is sometimes referred to as Catholic Neo-Pentecostalism. "Neo" comes from the Greek word "neos" meaning young or new. Therefore, Neo-Pentecostalism refers to the recent appearance of Pentecostalism in many of the major and more traditional religious groupings in the United States. Roman Catholicism is just one of these traditional religious groupings in which it has appeared. Others experiencing Pentecostalism infiltrating their ranks are the Episcopalian, the Lutheran, the Presbyterian, and in some parts of the country, the Baptists.[13]

It must be pointed out that the appearance of Pentecostalism within Roman Catholicism has not resulted in movement out of Catholicism on the part of those who have had the Pentecostal experience. Rather, it has served to add a certain amount of vitality to a rather reserved religious tradition. The majority of Roman Catholics who receive this baptism of the Holy Spirit do not leave the Roman Catholic church nor do they have any intention of doing so. They don't see Pentecostalism as undermining the Roman Catholic faith, but rather enhancing it by making it more appealing.[14]

Equally as interesting is the fact that the majority of the Roman Catholic leadership supports this new dimension of expressing the Roman Catholic faith. Bishop Alexander Zaleski of Lansing, Michigan issued the following statement in November 1969, a little more than two years after Pentecostalism initially infiltrated the Roman Catholic church.

There are many indications that this participation leads to a better understanding of the role the Christian plays in the church. Many have experienced progress in their spiritual life. They are attracted to the Scriptures and a deeper understanding of their faith.[15]

Pope Paul IV, while addressing a college of cardinals in 1973, made these comments about the Catholic Pentecostal movement now some six years old.

> The fresh breath of the Spirit . . . has come to awaken latent energies within the church, to stir up dormant charisms, and to infuse a sense of vitality and joy which makes the church youthful and relevant in every age, and prompts her to joyously proclaim her eternal message to each new epoch.[16]

Undoubtedly, the pope was well pleased with what was taking place within the Roman Catholic church as a result of the introduction and dissemination of Pentecostalism within its ranks.

In summary, then, the Neo-Pentecostal movement in the Roman Catholic church has been received with open arms on the part of the Roman Catholic leadership. It is regarded as a helpful expression for the welfare of the Roman Catholic church and its people. Indicative of this fact is its overwhelming acceptance by the people and its rapid development throughout the United States and other countries.

The Manifestation of Catholic Pentecostalism

The manifestations of Pentecostalism in the Roman Catholic church are certain supernatural "charisma" or gifts of the Holy Spirit. The basis or means by which these gifts are manifested in the life of the individual is the experience of the "Baptism of the Holy Spirit" previously alluded to in this chapter.

Before we examine these manifestations or gifts of the Spirit, we must first determine just exactly what the Roman Catholic means by the "Baptism of the Spirit." To determine this, as well as to examine the gifts of the Spirit which are said to be manifested in the Roman Catholic church, we will refer to a book by Father Vincent M. Walsh who is the Vice Chancellor of the Archdiocese of the Roman Catholic Church of Philadelphia. His book is entitled *A Key to Charismatic Renewal in the Catholic Church*. It is an important book to examine at this point because it, too, bears the imprimature of the Roman

Catholic church which indicates that it contains official Roman Catholic teaching.

The Baptism of the Spirit

Father Walsh defines the baptism of the Spirit in the following way. It is the divine act—

> whereby the individual experiences the risen Christ in a personal way. The experience results from a certain "release" of the power of the Holy Spirit, usually already present within the individual by Baptism and Confirmation. It usually leads to a deep devotional life, an attraction to prayer, Sacred Scripture, and the sacraments, and marks the beginning of a closer union with God.[17]

According to this definition, the baptism of the Spirit does not necessarily take place at the point of salvation. Of course the Roman Catholics would maintain a much different position on how personal salvation is achieved by mankind than we would as evangelicals. But for our purposes here, it is quite plain that the Roman Catholics in general see no connection between the baptism of the Spirit and the divine act of God whereby a sinner is reconciled to God through the shed blood of the Lord Jesus Christ.

Furthermore, on the basis of Father Walsh's definition, it is implied that not every "Christian" experiences the baptism of the Spirit. This must be the case since it is obvious that not every Christian experiences this "closer union with God." It is also true because certain conditions must be met in order to receive this baptism of the Spirit. Father Walsh lists these conditions as follows:

1. The individual must have a knowledge of the Baptism of the Holy Spirit.

2. The individual must have faith in the promise of Jesus to baptize in His Spirit.

3. The individual must experience repentance, sorrow for sin and a desire to do better.

4. The individual must experience some "reaching out for," "desire for," and "openness" to this fuller life in the Spirit.

5. The individual must participate in praying and sharing regularly with others who have received the gift of the Spirit.

6. The individual must experience being prayed with by others for the Baptism of the Spirit.[18]

These are very well-defined conditions for receiving the baptism of the Holy Spirit. It is implied that these conditions must be present in order for an individual to receive the baptism of the Holy Spirit regardless of what his relationship may be to God. The only problem with these conditions is that they have no basis in Scripture. Nowhere in Scripture is it stated that any of these conditions must be present in order to be baptized by the Holy Spirit.

Father Walsh is quick to point out, however, that the baptism of the Holy Spirit experienced by some Roman Catholics today is not exactly the same as the baptism of the Holy Spirit presented in Scripture. Regarding this he makes this statement:

> In Pentecostalism, the term has a very specialized use, referring to an internal religious experience, which usually initiates a life of fervor and results in the gift of prayer tongues. In Scripture the phrase (Baptism of the Holy Spirit) refers to the total gift of the Holy Spirit and not merely this one aspect of religious experience.[19]

Roman Catholic baptism of the Holy Spirit, then, is regarded as just one aspect of the total gift of the Holy Spirit. However, Scripture makes no distinction between these two kinds of baptisms of the Holy Spirit. This fact will be discussed in more detail later on in this chapter.

The Gifts Resulting from the Baptism of the Holy Spirit

Once an individual has received the baptism of the Holy Spirit as it is defined in Roman Catholic teaching, certain gifts are bestowed by the Spirit upon that individual. These gifts include ten major types or kinds. However, Father Walsh points out that it is actually impossible to determine exactly how many gifts of the Spirit there are.[20]

Prayer tongues: The first of these supernatural gifts is prayer tongues. It is implied that all who have been baptized by the Holy Spirit possess this gift. Furthermore, it is a permanent gift and it is usually the first gift bestowed by the Holy Spirit. As a result, it becomes the "doorway to the other gifts," according to Father Walsh.[21]

The nature or character of the gift of prayer tongues is expressed in two general ways. First of all, the individual exercising the gift of prayer tongues prays in a language which he does not know. He simply yields to the action of the Spirit. Secondly, He does not use rational powers of memory or intellect in exercising this gift. He only uses his lips, tongue, and larynx.[22]

Furthermore, no one who hears the individual praying in tongues understands what is being said, and the individual praying in tongues himself does not understand what he is saying.[23] In fact, Father Walsh points out that the gift of prayer tongues has no "rational purpose, in the sense of being used to communicate ideas to other minds."[24]

Speaking in tongues: The gift of speaking in tongues is said to be distinct from the gift of prayer tongues in Roman Catholic Pentecostalism. It is not necessarily possessed by all who have received the baptism of the Holy Spirit, and unlike prayer tongues it must be followed by the companion gift of interpretation.

The tongues that are spoken may be either known languages or they may be merely ecstatic utterances.[25] This gift, along with the gift of healing, seems to be the more prevalent of the charismatic gifts in Roman Catholic Pentecostalism.

Interpretation: As has already been mentioned, interpretation is the companion gift to the gift of speaking in tongues. The individual who possesses this gift is encouraged not to be afraid of it, but rather to train himself to freely speak whatever comes to his mind after having heard another individual speak in tongues.[26]

Prophecy: Father Walsh defines this gift as the "gift whereby God manifests to man His own thoughts so that a message may be given for the individual, or for a group of individuals, or for the community." What is implied by this definition is that those who possess the gift of prophecy are the recipients of new and actual revelations from God, which are the exact expression of the mind of God. In support of this, Father Walsh cites Old Testament and New Testament accounts of prophetic utterances.[27]

Healing: The gift of healing is said to be manifested in any one of three ways. It may be manifested in the form of physical healing to an individual with a physical ailment or sickness. It can also be manifested in the form of psychological healing to someone with emotional or mental problems.

Finally, it may be manifested in the form of spiritual healing. This type of healing involves the removal of an habitual sin or temptation to sin. In order to prove the validity of the gift of healing, Father Walsh appeals to the healing acts of Jesus Christ and the apostles recorded in the Gospels and the book of Acts in the New Testament.[28]

Faith: This gift is defined as the gift whereby the individual who possesses it "is enabled, without human reasoning or any sense of doubt on any level to ask or to speak in the name of Jesus in such a way that what he says or asks must come to pass." It is implied that this individual can predict the future due to his supernatural faith. Not only will he receive what he prays for, but what he says will actually come to pass.[29]

Miracles: This gift is defined by Father Walsh as the gift whereby "some obstacle is removed or some opportunity seized in a very special way, so that the effects must come from God's intervention into human affairs." Some examples of the results of the exercise of this gift include the instant healing of a disease, the complete change of mind by an individual to authority, the sudden conversion of an enemy of the church, the movement of physical objects so they can be found, and the sudden removal or arrival of a person so that problems are solved or opportunities taken.[30]

Discernment of spirits: This gift involves the ability of the person who possesses it "to see through the outward appearance of an action or inspiration in order to judge its source." The source may be from God, or from man, or from the devil, according to Father Walsh.[31]

The word of wisdom: This gift enables the person who possesses it "to give active, directive, or practical teaching which is an instrument of God for the hearers." In other words, this individual knows what is best in all situations. His advice and direction can always be counted on because he possesses the gift of the word of wisdom.[32]

The word of knowledge: This gift is said to be closely related to the gift of the word of wisdom. However, the gift of the word of knowledge enables the individual "to explain divine truths with clarity and unction." These divine truths may be either from the Holy Scriptures or from the sacred documents of the Roman Catholic church. Both are considered to be equally authoritative by the Roman Catholic church and therefore in need of explanation "with clarity and unction." Here the gift of the word of knowledge is to serve its purpose.[33]

The Scriptures and Roman Catholic Pentecostalism

Many examples could be cited to show that the Roman Catholic Pentecostal movement is inconsistent and contradictory to the teachings of Scripture. But the basic problem lies at the very root of Roman Catholic Pentecostalism and even Pentecostalism in general. This problem involves the misuse of Scripture and there is, therefore, an improper understanding of the baptism of the Holy Spirit.

As has already been seen, Roman Catholic teaching specifies that the baptism of the Holy Spirit is not necessarily connected with salvation. Rather, it is experienced by "Christians" after they've met certain conditions. These conditions, in general, involve certain acts of obedience on the part of the individual who wishes to be baptized by the Holy Spirit. Therefore, not every "Christian" is baptized by the Holy Spirit.

This is in direct contradiction to the teaching of the apostle Paul in 1 Corinthians 12:13. Here Paul specifically states "For by one Spirit are we all baptized into one body, whether we be Jews or Gentiles. . . ." The "all" here refers to all believers, all who have put their faith and trust in Jesus Christ as their Lord and Savior. No believer who truly is a believer is exempt from the baptism of the Holy Spirit.

Furthermore the tense of the Greek verb in this verse indicates a once-and-for-all act. The believer experiences the Baptism of the Holy Spirit immediately upon believing in Christ and it need not be repeated.

The purpose of the baptism of the Holy Spirit is also greatly misunderstood by most Roman Catholics. Its purpose is not to specifically bestow supernatural gifts upon those experiencing it. Rather, its purpose is to place the believer into the Body of Christ. As believers we have been made one with all other believers in the Church, which is the Body of Christ, by the baptism of the Holy Spirit.

Most Roman Catholics seek to justify this obvious contradiction with Scripture by stating that the baptism of the Holy Spirit experienced today is just one aspect of the total gift of the Spirit. However, as has already been pointed out, no such distinction is made in Scripture. The filling ministry of the Holy Spirit is distinct from the baptism of the Holy Spirit. But the filling ministry does not result in the manifestation of gifts of the Spirit. Therefore, this cannot be the baptism of the Holy Spirit taught by Roman Catholicism.

The only possible conclusion based on Scripture is that Roman Catholic Pentecostalism at its very root errs from the truth of Holy Scripture. The baptism of the Holy Spirit is not something to be sought or achieved, but rather it is the result of faith in Jesus Christ. Therefore, it is the experience of all true believers and not just those who are more obedient than others (1 Cor. 12:13; Eph. 4:5).

It should also be pointed out that the Roman Catholic Pentecostal movement thrives on experiences that are expressed by outward emotionalism. It is appealing because it serves to heighten the emotional and mental state of the people involved.[34] People in general are hungry for anything that will satisfy and fill the voids of life. The emotional climate surrounding Roman Catholic Pentecostalism helps to fill this void. The main problem is that at best it is but temporary. The only thing that will permanently fill the voids of life is a genuine personal relationship with the Lord Jesus Christ through faith in Him and Him alone. Emotionalism is a poor foundation for the Christian life. The only sure foundation is the knowledge gained of Christ from Holy Scripture.

As far as the specific gifts of the Spirit are concerned, the debate continues as to just exactly which gifts are permanent and which terminated at the end of the apostolic age. Without entering fully into the debate we can make these comments concerning the gifts of the Holy Spirit.

First of all, the gifts of the Holy Spirit, as they occurred in the apostolic period, served to accomplish one purpose. That purpose was to substantiate the message of the apostles and those who believed on Christ in regards to the mystery of the Church. Specifically, tongues were to be a sign to those who did not believe according to 1 Corinthians 14:22. The manifestation of tongues was to be a sign to the unbelieving Jews that God was now going to work through the Church or all those who had put their faith in Jesus Christ for eternal salvation.

Hebrews 2:3 and 4 further substantiate this fact. There the apostle Paul writes, "How shall we escape, if we neglect so great salvation;

which at the first began to be spoken by the Lord, and was confirmed unto us by them that heard him; God also bearing them witness, both with signs and wonders, and with divers miracles, and gifts of the Holy Ghost, according to His own will?" These gifts bore witness of the truth of the apostles. In God's plan it was necessary for such miraculous things to take place in order to clearly convince the unbeliever that what was taking place at the time of the apostles was not a fake or merely an emotional experience. The gospel message was genuine and the beginning of the Church, consisting of both believing Jew and Gentile, was genuine.

There is no need for such gifts of the Holy Spirit today. The Church and the gospel message have long since been substantiated. What's more, the canon of Holy Inspired Scripture has been completed. There is no need to seek further revelation from God by the use of charismatic gifts as practiced in Roman Catholic Pentecostalism. Needless to say, we have our hands full discerning and practicing the revelation of God as recorded in His Word, the Bible. The Church has reached a maturity in which there is no longer the need for such gifts of the Holy Spirit. In connection with this Paul said in 1 Corinthians 13:11, "When I was a child, I spake as a child, I understood as a child, I thought as a child: but when I became a man, I put away childish things." The Church today needs to become more excited about the Word of God and what the Holy Spirit can do in our lives through a knowledge of the truth of God's Word.

In conclusion, it is quite easy to see that Roman Catholic Pentecostalism and all that pertains to it has no real basis in Scripture. It emphasizes that which serves no real purpose in the Church today. An interesting observation is that in the pastoral epistles of the New Testament, written after Acts and 1 Corinthians, there is virtually no mention of the gifts of tongues, healings, etc. This is significant since Acts and 1 Corinthians were written quite early after the Church began. This further substantiates that these gifts were used less and less. Today, as believers, we must be involved in a diligent study of God's Word. Only by this can we know God's will for our lives. Only by this can we enjoy a close relationship with God. Nothing can take the place of God's Word, not even the modern day practices of Roman Catholic Pentecostalism.

1. Tugwell, Simon, *Did You Receive the Spirit?* (London: Darton, Longman & Todd, 1972), pp. 50–65.

2. Ibid., pp. 40–49.

3. Ibid.

4. Laurentin, Rene, *Catholic Pentecostalism* (Garden City, New York: Image Books, 1977), pp. 21, 22.

5. Ibid., pp. 22, 23.

6. Ibid., p. 23.

7. Ibid., pp. 23, 24.

8. Ibid., pp. 13, 14.

9. Ibid., p. 14.

10. Ibid., pp. 14, 15.

11. Ibid., pp. 15, 16.

12. Ibid., pp. 16–18.

13. Ibid., p. 24.

14. Ibid., pp. 24, 25.

15. Theological Digest 19 (1971), pp. 52, 53.

16. Pope Paul VI, Address to College of Cardinals, December 21, 1973 at Grottaferrata, Italy.

17. Walsh, Rev. Vincent M., *A Key to Charismatic Renewal in the Catholic Church* (St. Meinrad, In.: Abbey Press, 1974), p. 35.

18. Ibid., p. 41.

19. Ibid., pp. 36, 37.

20. Ibid., p. 67.

21. Ibid., p. 52.

22. Ibid., p. 51.

23. Ibid., p. 56.

24. Ibid., p. 54.

25. Ibid., pp. 82–92.

26. Ibid.

27. Ibid., pp. 96–116.

28. Ibid., pp. 120–141.

29. Ibid., pp. 144–150.

30. Ibid., pp. 150–157.

31. Ibid., pp. 160–173.

32. Ibid., pp. 176–182.

33. Ibid., pp. 182–189.

34. Gelpi, Donald L., *Pentecostalism: A Theological Viewpoint* (New York: Paulist Press, 1972), pp. 4–8.

7 / Ecumenism

James R. Lytle

. . . the Lord of Ages wisely and patiently follows out the plan of His
grace on behalf of us sinners. In recent times He has begun to bestow
more generously upon divided Christians remorse over their divisions,
and a longing for unity. Everywhere, large numbers have felt the impulse
of this grace, and among our separated brethren also there increases
from day to day a movement fostered by the Holy Spirit, for the
restoration of unity among all Christians.[1]

The Vatican II document on the "Decree of Ecumenism" begins
with these above words. In a world of diverse religions, a movement
has begun to unify the religious convictions of the people of the human
race. As the Vatican II documents attest, this movement has as its
hallmark a desire for unity centered upon those "who invoke the
Triune God and confess Jesus as Lord and Savior."[2] The Vatican II
documents welcome the ecumenical movement.

Unity is the central issue of ecumenism. "Oneness" is a most
difficult reality to attain, given the fractured state of Christianity. It is
even more difficult to attain when one considers the magnitude of the
concessions which must be made by certain parties if unity will exist.
Much of what has been precious doctrine—some of it established in the
blood of its first confessor—must be changed if ever there is hope of a
genuine unity in Christendom.

The Roman Catholic church is the last place in which one would
expect to find talk of ecumenism and unity. In the statements quoted
many times from the Documents of Trent, there is no room for
compromise of Catholic doctrine. After each of the statements of the
Council of Trent, the canons make clear the absolute nature of the

pronouncements of the council. The frequent usage of the term "anathema" consigned those who did not concur to the letter with the Roman position to hell.

One may also marvel at a Catholic call for ecumenism when one considers the identity of those with whom the Catholic must unite. The three sessions of the Council of Trent were called to forge orthodox doctrine in the face of the challenge of the Protestant Reformation. The people who received the "anathema" of the Council of Trent are the very ones who must now come to dialogue with the church which consigned them and their beliefs to hell!

The fundamentalists have long decried the ecumenical movement. The thought of compromise of doctrine is repugnant to those who hold to the authority of the Word of God. If doctrine is derived directly from the pages of the Scripture, and is not the invention of men, then there is no possibility of a compromise of belief. Fundamentalists will not be meeting Roman Catholics around the table for ecumenical dialogue.

Nevertheless, it is important for the fundamentalist to be aware of the Roman Catholic position on ecumenism. It is vital that understanding of the Roman Catholic position arise from the best of source materials. Though he may never dialogue with the Roman Catholic, the fundamentalist can gain a crucial perspective on the Roman church through their statements on ecumenism.

The Council of Trent had been singularly narrow in its view of salvation. Based on Trent, one would conclude that salvation was only to be found in the Roman Catholic church. In the Vatican II Decree on Ecumenism, the Roman Catholic church has affirmed that position, and supplies some basic principles on ecumenical participation.

First, the Roman Catholic church has recognized John 17:21 ("That they may all be one;") as a call for Christian unity. Unity has as its source the work of the Holy Spirit.[3] The work of the Holy Spirit is evidenced in the actions of the "College of the Twelve."[4] Through the action of these "faithful bishops" who succeeded Peter and the Twelve—in the administration of the sacraments, and exercise of authority—the people of Christ increase in the influence of the Holy Spirit, and thereby also increase in unity.[5] "The Church, then, God's only flock, like a standard lifted high for the nations to see, ministers the gospel of peace to all mankind . . . this is the sacred mystery of the unity of the Church."[6]

The primary principle of Roman Catholic ecumenism is that true unity lies in the church at Rome! Because of the succession of the bishops and the repository of truth in the church, it is the primary place of the Spirit's work. For the Catholic ecumenicist, unity does not require a great change in doctrinal belief, but the submission of others to the doctrine of his church.

A second principle which affects unity is the removal of the "sin of separation."[7] This sin was committed by the reformers when they left the church at Rome. This act of the reformers is not to be imputed by the modern Catholic to the descendents of the reformers. "The Catholic Church accepts them with respect and affection as brothers. For men who believe in Christ and have been properly baptized are brought into a certain, though imperfect, communion with the Catholic Church."[8]

The issue of faith is joined to the issue of baptism in the quote above. The sacrament of baptism is ultimately the determining factor in the "brotherhood" of Christians. For proper fellowship, the Roman church requires participation in Roman baptism. This basic principle is not meant to demean the erring brethren. "For the Spirit of Christ has not refrained from using them as means of salvation which derive their efficacy from the very fulness of grace and truth entrusted to the Catholic Church."[9] The fact that non-Catholics can experience salvation is based on the "overflow" of God's grace from the Roman Catholic church to the world at large. God is not working directly with the non-Catholic; the separated brethren merely receive benefits through the abundant blessing to the Roman Catholic church.

Lest there be any doubt, the framers of Vatican II documents included the following statement regarding their basic principles of ecumenism: "For it is through Christ's Catholic Church alone, which is the all-embracing means of salvation, that the fullness of the means of salvation can be obtained."[10] The Roman Catholic church approaches the issue of dialogue with a determination that the other must move!

The quotation above included the word "Catholic" between "Christ's" and "Church." The note was inserted on the express order of Pope Paul VI.[11] This is significant; since Catholic means "universal," the Pope wished to communicate that Christ's universal church has already been established. The remainder of the world, if it has hope of finding the universal church, need only seek the existing one.

With these two basic principles (*unity is caused by the Spirit's work through the Roman church, and salvation is based in Rome alone*), the Catholic is urged to participate "skillfully" in the work of ecumenism.[12]

> When such actions are carried out by the Catholic faithful with prudence, patience, and the vigilence of their spiritual shepherds, they contribute to . . . the spirit of brotherly love and unity. The result will be that, little by little, as the obstacles to perfect ecclesiastical communion are overcome, all Christians will be gathered, in a common celebration of the Eucharist, into that unity of the one and only Church which Christ bestowed on His Church from the beginning. This unity, we believe, dwells in the Catholic Church as something she can never lose, and we hope that it will continue to increase until the end of time.[13]

Little more need be said about the Roman Catholic church's perspective on ecumenism. In its ecumenical principles and in its ecumenical philosophy, the Roman Catholic church has denied the basic principles of ecumenical dialogue. The only reason for talking with the "separted brethren" is to make them unseparated! The fundamentalist should nonetheless be advised that the basic stance of the Roman Catholic church has not changed a bit. The Roman Catholic church still regards itself as the standard for truth and the repository of salvation.

In what manner might the Roman Catholic be directed to participate in ecumenical concerns? In accord with the others who are involved in ecumenism, the Roman Catholic church asserts that a "change of heart" is necessary for "ecumenism worthy of the name."[14] For the Roman Catholic, this "change of heart" does not involve changing views about a stated doctrine of the church. Instead, he should strive for purity of life *within* the Roman faith. "Let all Christ's faithful remember that the more purely they strive to live according to the gospel, the more they are fostering and even practicing Christian unity."[15]

In the process of individual strengthening in the faith, the Roman Catholic church is allowed a limited communion with the Protestant ecumenist. This may occur in the form of common prayer, but common worship must not be used "indiscriminately."[16] This serves to eliminate the danger of any of the Roman faithful being affected by the doctrines of an errant faith.

Education is also a part of Roman Catholic ecumenism. The Documents of Vatican II call for the "understanding" of the views of the separated brethren.[17] Study in the theological disciplines of the "separated brethren" will aid the Catholic to see the perspective from which the others involved in ecumenical dialogue argue. The Roman Catholic's role in ecumenical dialogue consists of the "more thorough" explanation of Roman beliefs.[18]

The prospect of dialogue with the sons of the Reformers poses special problems. Recognizing this, the Roman Catholic church has established a basic standard from which all such dialogue must be directed. "Baptism, therefore, constitutes a sacramental bond of unity linking all who have been reborn by means of it."[19] This is a rather stringent line of demarcation. Because of the potential difficulty in obtaining Protestant accord with the necessity of baptism to unity, the Roman Catholic church suggested another area for the beginning of ecumenical dialogue—moral questions. Though the sacrament of baptism would be divisive, certainly there could be unity and cooperation in the areas of social concern. This could lead to further fruitful discussion with the separated brethren.

One of the final statements in the section on ecumenism serves as a fitting summation of the Roman Catholic view of the issue.

> . . . ecumenical activity must not be other than fully and sincerely Catholic, that is, loyal to the truth we have received from the apostles and the Fathers, and in harmony with the faith which the Catholic Church has always professed, and at the same time tending toward that fullness with which our Lord wants His body to be endowed in the course of time.[20]

This statement does not leave anything to the imagination. Nothing has changed in the intention of the church since the time of the "anathemas" of the Council of Trent. The only possible move toward unity is the move that *other* ecumenists might make to attach themselves to the church at Rome. That church is committed to the concept that they are the final and true authority.

If the essential message and intention of the Roman church has not changed over the course of the years, then what is the purpose in considering the Roman Catholic's view of ecumenism? Simply stated, the concern involves the tactical change to be used by the Roman church to achieve its ends. In the speech which opened the council, Pope John XXIII made the follow statement:

> The church as always opposed . . . errors. Frequently she has condemned them with the greatest severity. Nowadays, however, the Spouse of Christ prefers to make use of the medicine of mercy rather than that of severity. She considers that she meets the needs of the present day by demonstrating the validity of her teaching rather than by condemnations. . . . That being so, the Catholic Church . . . desires to show herself to be the loving mother of all . . . She opens the fountain of her life-giving doctrine . . .[21]

Though he may never participate in ecumenical dialogue, the fundamentalist should be aware that the Roman Catholic church, which holds to another gospel, has changed its method of attack against the truth. The frontal attack has been replaced by one much more subtle, and much more difficult to counteract. Now as never before, the committed Christian must be able to quickly and accurately articulate the truths of the Word of God. Through ecumenical participation the Roman Catholic church will be attempting to educate others away from the truth of the Word. Someone must stand for the truth by boldly proclaiming the truth of God's Word.

1. Abbott, pp. 341, 342.
2. Ibid.
3. Ibid., p. 344.
4. Ibid.
5. Ibid.
6. Ibid.
7. Ibid., p. 345.
8. Ibid.
9. Ibid., p. 346.
10. Ibid.
11. Ibid.
12. Ibid., p. 347.
13. Ibid., p. 348.
14. Ibid., p. 351.
15. Ibid.
16. Ibid., p. 352.
17. Ibid., p. 353.
18. Ibid., p. 354.
19. Ibid., p. 364.
20. Ibid., p. 365.
21. Ibid., p. 716.

Glossary

ABSOLUTION: The Roman church has assigned the power to forgive sins to the priest, based on Matthew 16:19. The Bible refers to Christ as the only One Who has the power to absolve sins (*Col. 1:13*).

BAPTISM: The Roman Catholic believes that baptism is a sacrament which removes the penalty of original sin. It is an act which imparts the initial grace of salvation.

BISHOP In the hierarchical church, the bishop rules a diocese, and is responsible for the spiritual condition of all in the diocese. He directs the ministry of the priests.

CANON: The Greek term *kanon* indicates a measuring rod or standard of correctness. The "canons" which accompanied the decrees of the Council of Trent were designed to show precise areas of obedience to the doctrines of the council.

CONFESSION: A verbal confession to a priest is an annual obligation for the Roman Catholic. The priest will absolve their sins, and prescribe a penance. It is to precede the participation of the Roman Catholic in the Eucharist.

DIOCESE: The area in which a bishop has jurisdiction.

ECUMENICAL: By derivation of the Greek word *oikoumene* it refers to a council which has delegates from the "whole world." As a modern movement, it is an attempt to join all the Christian religious bodies of the world into one unified body. Non-Christian religions were at first not included in the movement, but have since been invited. The Catholic church is officially an outsider to the movement, awaiting the return of the Protestants to the Roman Church.

EUCHARIST: Eucharist is an equivalent term to the Lord's Supper,

Holy Communion, or Lord's Table. The Catholic understanding of the term supposes the transformation (*transubstantiation*) of the bread and wine into the actual body and blood of Christ. The Baptist views the supper as a memorial of the death of Christ.

EXTREME UNCTION: This sacrament, now renamed "anointing of the sick," was established by the Council of Trent as a preparation for death. It removes the penalty for any sins committed since the last confession.

FUNDAMENTALISM: This conservative movement came into being in response to the liberal theological movement of the nineteenth and twentieth centuries. In distinction to liberal teachers and pastors, the conservatives held to the "fundamental" doctrines of Christianity. The term is now more loosely applied to any conservative Protestant.

LATERAN COUNCILS: Between 1123 and 1512, five councils were convened in the church of St. John Laterine in Rome. The councils were designed to enhance the unity and authority of the Roman church. They proved to be a battleground between the popes and the cardinals, and attempted to protect the papacy from European rulers. An occasional attempt to reform was suggested.

MASS: The Roman church views the Mass as a literal sacrifice of Christ for the sins of the parishioners. The actual body and blood of Christ are offered as a sacrifice for sins when the elements of the Eucharist are changed from bread and wine to Christ's body and blood. The doctrine developed during the latter Middle Ages, and was declared to be true by the Council of Trent.

PRIEST: In the Bible, the priest ministered the sacrifices of men to God. The position of the priesthood in the Christian church developed in the early centuries of the church, and became well established in the Middle Ages. The existence of the priesthood assumes that sacrifice is still being offered on behalf of men. This is denied by Hebrews 10:14.

REFORMATION: This general term refers to the early attempts of European Catholics to restore purity to the Catholic church. As time passed and the objective of restoring purity became impossible to obtain, the term came to refer to any person who held to doctrines contrary to the Roman faith. The doctrine of justification by faith alone was a hallmark of the Reformation.

SACRAMENT: A sacrament is an action or activity which channels grace to man. In the Roman church, seven different activities provide grace for man: baptism, confirmation, Eucharist, holy orders, marriage, extreme unction (*anointing of the sick*) and penance.

SCHOLASTICISM: The predominant theological/philosophical movement of the eleventh to fourteenth centuries, scholasticism, emphasized the unity of philosophy and theology. Aristotle's Greek philosophy was joined to Christian revelation. Reason became an important adjunct to faith. The Renaissance, humanism and the Reformation worked toward the downfall of this medieval science.

TRANSUBSTANTIATION: The sacrifice of the Mass effects the change of the bread and wine into the body and blood of Christ. Although no change is evident in the bread and wine, it is nonetheless a genuine change of substance.

TRENT, COUNCIL OF: This council was designed to counter the Protestant Reformation. It met in three stages (*1545–47, 1551–52, 1562–63*), and clarified the larger portion of Roman Catholic doctrine. This council set the number of sacraments at seven, and defined the doctrine of the Mass more precisely.

VATICAN II: This Second Vatican Council (*Vatican I, 1870*) was called by Pope John XXIII in 1962 (*1962–65*). In the four sessions, the council modernized the Catholic faith, allowed for the observance of the Mass in the vernacular and opened the door for the return of the Protestants (*separated brethren*) to Rome. The council did not change any prior Catholic doctrine.

Bibliography

General Works

Abbott, Walter, ed. *The Documents of Vatican II.* New York: The America Press, 1966.

Aquina, Thomas. *On the Truth of the Catholic faith.* 3 vols. Garden City: Doubleday & Co., 1955.

Augustine, *Treatises on Marriage and Other Subjects.* New York: Fathers of the Church, Inc., n.d.

Bainton, Roland. *Here I Stand.* Nashville: Abingdon-Cokesbury Press, MCML.

Bartlett, John R. *Rist and Second Books of the Maccabees.* New York: Cambridge University Press.

Benedict, Saint. *The Dialogues of Gregory the Great.* New York: Bobbs-Merrill Company, Inc.

Boettner, Loraine. *Roman Catholicism.* Philadelphia: Presbyterian and Reformed Publishing Co., 1962.

Bokenkotter, Thomas. *A Concise History of the Catholic Church.* Garden City: Doubleday & Co., 1977.

Chemnitz, Martin. *Examination of the Council of Trent.* 2 vols. Translated by Fred Kramer. St. Louis: Concordia Publishing House, 1978.

Chiniquy, Charles. *Fifty Years in the Church at Rome.* Sea Cliff: Christ's Mission Book Dept., 1953.

Dolan, John P. *Catholicism.* Woodbury, New York: Barrows Educational Series, 1968.

Douglas, J.D., gen. ed. *The New International Dictionary of the Christian Church.* Grand Rapids: Zondervan Publishing House, 1974.

Dulles, Avery. *The Resilient Church.* New York: Doubleday & Co., 1977.

Elliott, Charles. *Delineation of Roman Catholicism.* London: Wesleyan Conference Office, 1877.

Fairweather and Black. *The First Book of Maccabees.* Cambridge: University Press, 1967.

Garver, Stuart. *Watch Your Teaching.* Hackensack, NJ: Christ's Mission, Inc., 1973.

Gelpi, Donald L. *Pentecostalism: A Theological Viewpoint.* New York: Paulist Press, 1972.

Guiness, H. Gratten. *Romanism and the Reformation.* London: Hodder and Stoughton, 1887.

Hardon, John A., *The Catholic Catechism.* Garden City, New York: Doubleday & Company, Inc., 1973.

Ketcham, R. T. *Let Rome Speak for Herself.* Chicago: Regular Baptist Press, 1956.

Laurentin, Rene. *Catholic Pentecostalism.* Garden City, New York: Image Books, 1977.

Marrow, Stanley B. *The Words of Jesus in Our Gospels.* New York: Paulist Press, 1979.

McKenzie, John L. *The Roman Catholic Church.* New York: Holt, Rinehart and Winston, 1964.

Neuner, Josef and DuPuis, J., eds. *The Christian Faith.* Westminster: Christian Classics, Inc., 1975.

Origen, *On First Principles.* Gloucester, Mass.: Peter Smith, n.d.

Pelikan, J. and Lehmann, H. *Luther's Works,* American Ed. Philadelphia and St. Louis, 1955.

Plato, *Plato on the Immortality of the Soul.* New York: Hurst & Company Pub., 1956.
Rahner, Karl, *Theological Investigations.* vol. 1: "God, Christ, Mary and Grace." London: Denton, Longman and Todd, 1974.
————. *Theological Investigations.* vol. 6: "Concerning Vatican Council II." London: Darton, Longman and Todd, 1974.
————. *Theological Investigations.* vol. 13: "Theology, Anthropology, Christology." New York: Seabury Press, 1975.
Roberts, Alexander and Donaldson, James, eds. *The Ante-Nicene Fathers.* 10 vols. Grand Rapids: Wm. B. Eerdmans Publishing Co., 1950.
Rone, Wendell. *The Baptist Faith and Roman Catholicism.* Kingsport, TN: Kingsport Press, 1952.
Schaff, Philip, ed. *The Nicene and Post Nicene Fathers.* 23 vols. Grand Rapids: Wm. B. Eerdmans Publishing Co., 1956.
————. *History of the Christian Church.* 8 vols. Grand Rapids: Wm. B. Eerdmans, 1910.
Schroeder, Rev. H. J. (O. P.), trans. *Canons and Decrees of the Council of Trent.* St. Louis, MO: B. Herder Book Co., 1941.
————. *Canons and Decrees of the Council of Trent.* London: B. Herder Book Co., 1941.
Standridge, William C. *Born-again Catholics and the Mass.* Greensboro, NC: Independent Faith Mission, 1980.
Tugwell, Simon. *Did You Receive the Spirit?* London: Darton, Longman and Todd, 1972.
Walsh, Rev. Vincent M. *A Key to Charismatic Renewal in the Catholic Church.* St. Meinrad, IN: Abbey Press, 1974.
Wathington, Amanda. *Christ Our Lord.* Wilmington, NC: McGrath Publishing, 1978.
Weimer. *Luther's Werke.* Kritische Gesamtausgabe, 1883ff.
Williams, Robert R. *A Guide to the Teachings of the Early Church Fathers.* Grand Rapids: Wm. B. Eerdmans, 1960.

Authority

Baum, Gregory. *Faith and Doctrine.* Paramus, NJ: Newman Press, 1969.
Dixon, A. C. *The True and the False.* Baltimore: Wharton, Barron & Co., 1890.
Macaulay, Joseph. *Truth vs. Dogma.* Chicago: Moody Press, 1946.
Megwern, James. *Bible Interpretation.* Wilmington, NC: McGrath Publishing Co., 1978.
Neuner, Josef. *The Teaching of the Catholic Church.* Cork: The Mercer Press, 1965.
Rahner, Karl and Ratzinger, Joseph. *Revelation and Tradition.* Dorval, Ontario: Palm Publishers, 1966.

Mass and Eucharist

Glavin, John F. *Following the Mass.* New York: Edward O'Toole Co., 1936.
Lovasik, Lawrence. *The Eucharist in Catholic Life.* New York: Macmillan Co., 1960.
————. *Modern Eucharistic Agreement.* London: SPCK, 1973.
Pittinger, Norman. *Life as Eucharist.* Grand Rapids: Wm. B. Eerdmans Publishing, 1973.
Powers, Jos. M. *Eucharistic Theology.* New York: The Seabury Press, 1967.
Schillebeechx, Edward. *The Eucharist.* New York: Sheed and Ward, 1968.
Walerman, Lucius. *The Primitive Tradition of the Eucharistic Body and Blood.* New York: Longmans, Green and Co., 1919.

Sacraments

Kung, Hans, ed. *The Sacraments: An Ecumenical Dilemma.* New York: Paulist Press, 1966.

Megivern, James. *Worship and Liturgy.* Wilmington, NC: McGrath Publishing Co., 1978.

Schillebeechx, Edward and Williams, Boniface, eds. *The Sacraments in General.* New York: Paulist Press, 1968.

Ecumenism

Berhouwer, G. C. *Recent Developments in Roman Catholic Thought.* Grand Rapids: Wm. B. Eerdman, 1958.

Fitzsimmons, Matthew, ed. *The Catholic Church Today: Western Europe.* Notre Dame: University Press, 1969.

Gurian, Waldemar and Fitzsimmons, M. A., eds. *The Catholic Church in World Affairs.* Notre Dame: University Press, 1954.

Kung, Hans, ed. *The Church and Ecumenism.* New York: Paulist Press, 1965.

Rahner, Karl. *The Church After the Council.* New York: Herder and Herder, 1966.

Schillebeechx, Edward. *The Mission of the Church.* New York: Seabury Press, 1973.

Weigel, Gustave. *Catholic Theology in Dialogue.* New York: Harper and Bros., 1960.

Westow, Theo. *Introducing Contemporary Catholicism.* Philadelphia: Westminster Press, 1967.

Articles and Other Publications

Pope Paul VI: Address to College of Cardinals, at Grottaferrata, Italy; December, 1973.

Second Council of Lyons: "Profession of Faith of Michael Palaeologus" Denzinger 464 (856).

General Association of Regular Baptist Churches: "Constitution and Articles of Faith of the General Association of Regular Baptist Churches." Des Plaines, Illinois: Regular Baptist Press, n.d.

"The Vatican: A Glimpse into the Papal Purse," *Business Week* (December 24, 1979): 52.

Theological Digest 19 (1971): 52, 53.